THE FORGOTTEN GOSPEL
OF ST. BARNABAS

THE FORGOTTEN GOSPEL

OF

ST. BARNABAS

DR. M.H. DURRANI

kitab bhavan

NEW DELHI-110 002. [INDIA]

KITAB BHAVAN

Publishers, Distributors, Exporters & Importers
1784, Kalan Mahal, Darya Ganj,
New Delhi - 1100 02 (India)

Phones :   (91-11) 23277392/93, 23274686, 32906494
Fax   :   (91-11) 23263383

Website :   www.nusratalinasri.com

Email   :   nasri@vsnl.com
         :   nusrat@bol.net.in

1st Print in India   :   1998
3rd Reprint in   :   2011

ISBN No.   :   81-7151-249-6
Book Code No.   :   F00045

Printed & Published in India by :
Nusrat Ali Nasri for KITAB BHAVAN
1784, Kalan Mahal, Darya Ganj,
New Delhi - 1100 02 [India]

CONTENTS

INTRODUCTION

Incessant search for Truth took me away from Christianity and brought me back, by the grace of Almighty Allah, Rahman and Rahim, to Islam, the religion of my fore-fathers.

For my coming back to the fold of Islam, the cause was the inspiration given to me through a dream wherein I seem to have been blessed with the personal blessings of the Holy Prophet (p.b.u.h.). I praise God and pray for His Holy Prophet (P.b.u.h.) and am overjoyed to find the Prophet (p.b.u.h.) who gave man his dignity and the freedom to act by his own choice.

Change of heart comes from Almighty God. In fact without His guidance, all our searching and all our efforts, however skilful to find the Truth, may lead us astray.

We need guiding vision and conviction without which no argument, however cogent, nor ay eloquence however impassioned, nor learning however deep, will ever make man satisfied unless he has the proof within his own soul. The only way to have it, is to receive it as a free gift from God Almighty, Most Gracious, Most Merciful.

Much has been said and written by the Christian Pontiffs about Jesus. His sayings and teachings are supposedly contained in the Four Gospels of the so-called Apostles, Canonized centuries after the Ascension of Jesus by the order of the Roman Emperor Constantine.

This happened in the year 325 C.E. In compliance will the imperial command two thousand and eight bishops assembled at Nicaea to debate, discuss and decide theological matters and also select, by common agreement, those books from a vast collection of manuscripts which, in their judgement, constituted the authorised word of God.

Now these bishop who were commanded by an Emperor to exercise judgement in determining the books that contained the word of God were all torn between worldly powers, personal ambition and ignorance. Sabinus, the learned bishop of Heraclea recorded that "excepting Constantine himself and Eusblus Pambhibus, they were a set of illiterate, simple creatures that understood nothing." Idiots as they were, Pappus recounts that "having promiscuously put all the books that were referred to the Council for determination under the communion table in the Church, they besought the Lord that the inspired writings might get upon the table, while the spurious one remained underneath."

(Sherman, H. You Live after Death, Ch.8)

Out of some fifty Gospels, then existent, only those of Mathew, Mark, Luke and John were selected. The rest were rejected. The Emperor then decreed that the above decision be considered as sanctioned by the Divine Will and that the above mentioned Four Gospels should implicit the word of God. He also ordered that the rejected manuscripts along with the writings of ARIUS be burnt and that anyone found to be possessing, concealing or otherwise preaching anything other than the authorised word of God shall be punished with death. All bishop bowed before the power. His Imperial Majesty Constantine, thus produce the first copy of New Testament.

Thomas Paine says:

" The Councils of Nicaea and Locodicea were held about 350 C.E. years after the time Christ, is said to have lived; and the books that now compose the New Testament were then voted for by AYES and NOES, as we now vote a law. A great many that were offered had a majority of NAYS and were rejected. This is the way the New Testament came into being". (Age of Reason, p. 92).

None of these Gospels however, separately or all collectively, gives an honest account of the whole life of Jesus, his sayings, teachings and doings. They are full of contradictions and anomalies, and even some Christian scholars have declared Jesus to be a Mythical personality contrary wise to the real historical Jesus, which Islam has authentically asserted to have been existed. Digest and confusion are inspired by the present day Christianity which was born out of the Constantine's system of democratically deciding to find the real Gospels out of the fifty presented in 325 C.E. The religion of Jesus, of course, is divine but the Gospels are not divine, they are man-made, approved by the majority of the Council of Nicaea gathered together under the orders of Constantine. Christianity has thus lost its Divine Character nor for one reason alone; but for many, because it is in total opposition to the Divine positions and teachings of God's Messengers sent to the people of the world, before the arrival of Jesus in the world.

The thirst for truth was not quenched. It remained increasing even when I was an ordained Priest of the Church of England, India, Ceylon and Pakistan. I had read and learnt about St. Barnabas, and also that the under the guidance of Jesus had declared Muhammad (p.b.u.h.) as the last Messiah in his Gospel. This Gospel was, however, condemned later on by the Pontiffs of Christianity, being in opposition and contrary to their own beliefs received from St. Paul— the de facto founder of Modern Christianity which centres around the doctrine of Trinity created by him.

Again and again I sat down to study the Gospels, Epistles and Acts of Apostles etc. on which Christianity is based and made a comparative study of the Gospels of St. Barnabas and the Four Gospels etc. I have recorded my empirical observation for Christians and Muslims both to learn the truth about St. Barnabas and his Gospel in my treatise "Gospel Vs. Gospels"— The truth about the "Lost Gospel"— Barnabas.

Human hands cannot replace the Divine Hand. Bags made by God cannot be replaced by man-made bags. The Divine revelation given to Jesus having lost purity in the New Testament is here for all to see for themselves. On this point Muir, in his book, 'Life of Muhammad', states as follows:

"The Christianity of the seventh century was itself decrepit and corrupt. It was disabled by contending schisms, and had substituted the puerilities of superstitions for the pure expensive faith of early ages."

I pray to Almighty Allah to bestow light on all human beings of the world and guide them to the right path of LIFE.

M. H. DURRANI

(1)

BARNABAS, -- 'APOSTLE AND PROPHET'

Barnabas, Christian Apostle and Prophet, a companion of St. Paul on some of his missionary journey*. Traditionally, he was Bishop of Milan, founded the Church at Antioch, and suffered martyrdom in Rome. His festival is June, 11. Several writings are attributed to him, in particular the "Epistle of Barnabas, which is included in the Codex Sinaiticus, and is addressed apparently to Christians, in danger of returning to Judaism."

> (*Encyclopaedia of Religion and Religion*
> by E. Rogston Pike, pp. 46).

His name was Joses, a Levite from Cyprus, he sold his land and liberally deposited all the price with the Apostle Incharge, for distribution among the poor, so that none was in want. The Apostles attached him very closely to themselves and called him Barnabas, which means the son of exhortation or consolotion.[1]

He was an intelligent and devoted man, and a facile speaker. He was numbered among the Apostles and Prophets.[2] Clement of Alexandria calls him one of the seventy disciples.[3] And also the Dictionary of Bible, says that "There is ancient authority for identifying him with one of the seventy disciples of our Lord", quoting Eusebius Bk. 1.12. Clement of Alexandria, *Mise or in Strom*. 11.20. He was the zealous disciple of Jesus".[4]

He was not only an inspired preacher, but also a writer. "An Epistle belonging to the late first or early second century is still extant, which has been ascribed to Barnabas

---

* *A History of Christianity in the Apostolic Age* by Arthur Cushman Meciffert, Ph.D. page 653.

1. *The Acts of the Apostles*, 4:36,37. See also *Compact Bible Dictionary*, p. 70.

2. *Acts of the Apostles*, 13:1

3. *Strom*. 11.20, see also the *Eusebius*, Bk. 1, Chap. 12.

4. Watts *Scripture History*, p. 284.

since the time of Clement of Alexandra."[5]

"There was clearly a great deal of writing by Christians in the period A.D. 60 to 160. In addition to our New Testament books, there were certainly three other documents that were read in the Churches. One of these first were the Epistle of Barnabas".[6]

With regard to the authorship of the Gospel of St. Barnabas, Roderic Dunkerly says: "It is known that there was an Apocryphal Gospel attributed to Barnabas in the FIFTH CENTURY."[7]

CHARACTERISTICS OF BARNABAS

(1) Title-Names Changed: Barnabas.

And Joses, who by the apostles was surnamed Barnabas (which is, being interpreted the son of consolation), a Levite, and of the country of Cyprus'. (Ac. 4: 36)

(2) Sacrificial Giving:

'Having land, sold it, and brought the money, and laid it at the apostles' feet'. (Ac. 4: 37).

(3) Broad Mindedness:

'Barnabas took him, (Paul) and brought him to the apostles, and declared unto them how he had seen the Lord in the way, and that he had spoken to them, and how he had preached bodly at Damascus in the name of Jesus.'

(AC. 9: 27).

(4) Gift of Exhortation:

.... and they sent forth Barnabas, that he should go as far as Antioch. Who, when he came, and had seen the grace of God, was glad, and exhorted them all.

(Ac. 11 : 22—23).

---

5. *The Apostolic Age*, p. 126.
6. *An Outline of Church History,* p. 68.
7. *Beyond the Gospel* p. 153.

(5) Spirit Filled:

'For he was good man, and full of the Holy Ghost and of faith; and much people was added unto the Lord.' (Ac.11:24)

(6) Inspiring influence:

'Then departed Barnabas to Tarsus for to seek Saul; and when he had found him, he brought him unto Antioch. And it came to pass, that a whole year they assembled themselves with the Church, and taught much people. And the disciples were called Christians first in Antioch'.

(Ac. 11 : 25, 26)

(7) Trustworthy:

'Then the disciples, every man according to his ability, determined to send relief unto the brethren which dwelt in Judaea which also they did, and sent it to the elders by the hands of Barnabas and Saul'. (Ac. 11: 29, 30).

(8) Fine Personal Appearance:

'And they called Barnabas, Jupiter.' (Ac. 14: 12).

(9) Adapted to Missionary Work:

'As they ministered to the Lord, and fasted, the Holy Ghost, said, separate me Barnabas.' (Ac. 13:2)

(10) Prophet:

'Now there were in the Church that was at Antioch certain prophets and teachers; as Barnabas, and Simeon that was called Niger, and Lucius of Cyrene, and Manaen which had been brought up with Herod the tetrach, and Saul. (Ac. 13:1)

In the light of the indisputable facts which have been presented in the Book of Acts, we come to the conclusion that as regards the personality of St. Barnabas, he was not only a man of unblemished character but also held high office in the Church as an Apostles and a Prophet.

Another significant fact is that St. Barnabas was appointed by Jesus himself to write the Gospel.

"And Jesus turned himself to him who writeth, and said: See, Barnabas, that by all means thou write my Gospel concerning all that happened through my dwelling in the world. And write in like manner that which hath befalled Judas, in order that the faithful may be undeceived, and every one may believe the truth".[8]

In our survey we have noticed that St. Barnabas was a real disciple and apostle of Jesus. But Drs. Jan Slomps has called him PSEUDO-BARNABAS[9] and has thus betrayed his frame of mind. It is most regrettable that even in these enlightened times people pay such regard in religious matters, to those comments and interpretations which they have heard and accepted without testing them on the criterion of reason. They, for example, accept that it is absolutely impossible for another Gospel to exist besides the Four recognised Gospels, though it is absolutely an absurd concept. In the Nicaea Council, a large number of Gospels were presented, including Peter's Gospel, the Gospel of Thomas, the Gospel of Barnabas, and his Epistles etc. Where are those Gospels now? Why does Anglican Church celebrate the Day of Barnabas every year.[10]

The Gospel of Barnabas is not a tough problem of mathematics that might confuse the minds — it is, on the contrary, as simple as to say that two and two make four. The same arguments used to prove the authenticity of the four Canonical Gospels go to prove the authenticity of even the Gospel of Barnabas, because the person of Barnabas is a recognized one.

Now, to deny such a personality would be similar to the denial of Peter who had denied his "Lord Thrice" and went so far as to curse him. Hence Drs. Jan Slomps, using

8. *Barnabas.* ccxxi.

9. *Pseudo — Barnabas,* in the context of Muslim-Christian Apolo-getics, Published by the Christian Study Centre, Rawalpindi.

10. The book of *"Common Prayer".* p.9, (Church of England).

his own yard stick, writes about "Pseudo Barnabas", instead of Saint Barnabas and makes no mention at all of the person of Pseudo Barnabas. If the Saint Barnabas and Pseudo Barnabas are the names of one and the same person, he should give the reasons for calling him "PSEUDO". The authenticity of the Gospel of Barnabas cannot be denied by pointing out the style of narration, the quality of paper or the contradictions, for the same measuring stick can also be applied to the Four Canonical Gospels, as they contain many examples, of contradictions, absurdity, immorality and indecency.

With regard to inspiration of the Gospels, Professor J. Volckaret S.J., says that "God, the author of the Gospels, does not actually execute the writing miraculously; for this purpose He avails Himself of man as an instrument; He uses the very individuality of the bibliography, his individual way of thinking, of expressing himself, his individual mentality. There is a very intimate cooperation between the action of God and the work of the bibliographer, God inspiring, influencing, building the free operation of His human instrument. In this way we understand quite well how God is the author of the Four Gospels yet each has its own very pronounced character as regards contents, scope and style."[11]

Mathew, Mark, Luke and John are all HUMAN. They are all subject to error. Even though they are directed, empowered and blessed by Him.

Thus, any concept that assumes God's TRUE WORK by a human is absolutely perfect, incapable of being wrong, or containing mistakes or errors, is a false and therefore will be misleading.

St. Augustine mentions this, in a letter to St. Jerome, when in the pages of Sacred writ : I came upon anything that is contrary to the truth, I judge that the text is faulty, that the translation did not strike the right meaning or simply that I do not understand it.[12]

For an adequate appreciation of the subject under discussion the following basic facts have to be clearly borne in mind:

---

11. *The Saviour:* Introduction of the Four Gospels(P.XII).
12. *Letter to St. Jerome* ixxx.3 (P. 11).

Firstly, the 'INJEEL', mentioned by the Holy Qur'an[13] is not the NEW TESTAMENT that consists of FOUR GOSPELS, ACTS, TWENTY-ONE EPISTLES and REVELATION.

Secondly, as the Holy Qur'an points out, as SCRIPTURE it has not value, because of its distortions and alterations, although HOLY QURAN recognised its written as inspired men of GOD, but their books, later, prove the alteration beyond all doubts.

Thirdly, the writers of the Four Gospels report in Greek the sayings of Jesus who spoke Aramaic. A copyist would sometimes put in not the text as it is but what he thought ought to be in it. He would trust a fickle memory, or he would even change the text according to the view of the school to which he belonged.

As Prof. F.C. Burkitt, says: "The Four Biographies of Jesus Christ......... are not all independent of each other, and neither of them was intended by its writer to form one of quartette. But they are all put side by side, unharmonised, one of them being actually imperfect at the end, and one being only the first volume of a larger work. All this body of unmethodical literature was casuals in its nature. No wonder, because the early Christians expected the end of the world very soon. The Four Canonical Gospels were only Four out of many, and some others besides the four have survived. Each writer just wrote down some odd sayings of the Master that he recollected. Among the miracles described there is only one which is described in all the four Gospels and others were described, and believed in, in others' Gospels, which are not mentioned in any of the FOUR Canonical Gospels. Some of the Epistles contain exposition of doctrine, but this has been interpreted differently by different churches.

There must have been hundreds of such Epistles, and not all the Epistles, now received as Canonical, were always so received or intended to be so received. The Apocalypse also was not the only one in the field. There were others. They were others. They were prophecies of "Things which must shortly come to pass;" they could not have been meant for long preservation,

---

13. *Al-Qur'an.*

"for the time is at hand."[14]

On close examination, however, it must be admitted that in its present form it is the work of man. I shall deal with this subject separately.

It is, however, clear that St. Barnabas was given the privilege and honour of writing the Gospel. Thus St. Barnabas tells under God's inspiration how he came to write the Gospel of Jesus. If you are looking for the REAL GOSPEL which claims that it is written under God's inspiration, that Gospel is the GOSPEL OF ST. BARNABAS.

---

14. See Prof. F.C. Burkitt on the *Canon of the New Testament, in Religion,* June 1934, the Journal of translations of the society of Promoting the study of Religions. See also R. W. Mackay, *Rise and Progress of Christianity,* G. R. S. Mead, *The Gospel and the Gospels;* B.W. Bacon, *Making of the New Testament, with Bibliography.*

(2)

ST. BARNABAS' DAY

SAYS THE REV. H.J. WILMOT-BUXTON
AUTHOR OF:
"THE OLD ROAD", "THE LIGHTS OF HOME",
"READING FOR MOTHER'S MEETINGS",
"MISSION SERMONS FOR AYGAR",
"SUNDAY LESSONS FOR DAILY LIFE",
"THE BATTLE OF LIFE DUTY",
"BY WORD AND DEED",
"THE LIFE WORTH LIVING",
"PRAYER AND PRACTICE",
"THE TREE OF LIFE",
"IN MAN KEYS",
"COMMON LIFE RELIGION",
"DAY BY DAY DUTY",
"BIBLE OBJECT LESSONS", ETC.

THE LIFE OF ST. BARNABAS

The ancestors of St. Barnabas, who were jews of the tribe of Levi, migrated to the island of Cyprus to escape the persecution of Gentile enemies. In Judaea a Levite was prohibited from acquiring landed property, but this law was not binding on the exiles, and St. Barnabas had secured or inherited an estate which he sold, and placed the price at the apostle's feet.

Receiving the name of Joses (a Hellenistic form of the favourite name Joseph) at his circumcision, he was sent as a young man to be educated at Jerusalem, under the famous teacher Gamaliel, and one of his fellow students was Saul of Tarsus. Thus began the friendship which in after years was to unite the two men as apostles in the work of Christ.

The occasion of the Call of St. Barnabas is not known, but he is supposed to have been one of the seventy disciples sent forth by Jesus. He was endowed by God with singular gifts. His power of consoling and comforting others gained him the name of the Son of consolanation. His singular beauty and majesty of form made the Greeks at Lystra mistake him for Jupiter, his eloquence was remarkable, and his wealth enabled him to comfort the poor and struggling members of the Church.

Such was the man who introduced his college friend, Saul of Tarsus, to the disciples, when they distrusted the converted persecutor of the Church. In his company St. Barnabas went on a missionary tour confirmation to the Church of Antioch, where the disciples were first called Christians. For a period of fourteen years two apostles worked together, and their mission ended, as it had begun, at Antioch. A dispute about retaining St. Mark in their company caused the parting of the friends, and St. Barnabas returned to his native Cyprus.

The future movements of St. Barnabas are uncertain. He is said to have visited Italy, and founded the Church of Milan. His last years were spent in Cyprus, where he laboured for the conversion of the Jewish colony there. Certain jews from Syria arrived in the island, and stirred up their brethren against the apostle. St. Barnabas, foreseeing the end, charged his nephew St. Mark, with a last message to his old friend St. Paul, and left instructions for his burial. Then he celebrated the Holy Encharist with the faitiful, and bade them farewell.

Next, he went to the synagogue as salamis, and ț reached the gospel of Jesus, but the jews seized him, stoned him to death, and attempted to burn his body, which, however, is said to have resisted the flames. St. Mark burried the body of his kinsman in a cave, and joined St. Paul, with whom he remained. Four hundred years after his martyrdom, the remains of the Son of Consolation were removed to Constantinople, by the Emperor Leno, who built a stately Church over them, and dedicated it to St. Barnabas.

St. Barnabas Our Example

St. Barnabas was a rich man, and he gave his wealth to the cause of the Church. We cannot all do that, because we are not all rich, but if we have little, we can do our best to give gladly of that little to the cause of religion. So of St. Barnabas is an example of self-denial. He was a man of many gifts, and he dedicated them to Christ. We all have some gifts, and we must try to use them in the service of the Master. St. Barnabas gave himself to God's service, we all do that in one way or another. Specially, he dedicated himself by being a son of consolation, by conforting and consoling his fellow-men. That is within the power of us all.

All Christians Should Be Sons of Consolation

St. Barnabas was, we are told, full of the Holy Ghost, and it was this which enabled him to be the son of consolation. We must be filled with the Holy Ghost, the comforter, if we are to be a comfort or consolation to our fellow-men. The man without religion never brought consolation to a sorrowful heart hungering after God.

This world is full of sad, lonely, suffering people, and it is the plain duty of all Christians to try to console them. The wayside of life is crowded by those who have fallen on the journey, and it is our part to act the part of the good Samaritan, and pour in the wine and oil of kindly help. We can comfort our brethren by[15] kind acts, a visit, a pleasant talk, the reading of a good book[16] by kind words, rudeness is as great a sin as cruelty[17], by sympathy — rejoice with them that do rejoice, and weep with them that weep.

Published in
"*Notes of the Sermons for the Year*"
By
Skeffington & Sons,
34 Southampion Street,
Strand, W.C. London.

---

15. Traditionally he was bishop of Milan, founded the Church of Antioch.
16. See also the page of this book. St. Barnabas wrote the teachings of Jesus under theinspirations i.e. the guidance of the Holy Ghost
17. Acts. 15:12 — "Barnabas speaks of the signs and wonders God had wrought among the Gentiles by them and in 28:9 concerning the healing of their in the Island of Malta. *Psychology Religions.*

(3)

REPUTATION OF CHRISTIAN
APOLOGETICAL ACCOUNT

Lie made lie. Jesus said: "Truth shall make you free"

Linsdale and Loura Ragg, Dr. Jan Slomp and also other Apologetics have judged the Gospel of Barnabas much more in the spirit of criticsm than that of research scholars, as all of them belong to the same school of thought; they accpeted the Four Canonical Gospels as true and have set the same as the criterion for testing the Gospel of St. Barnabas; They quote references not from History but from their own school of sweet thought which renders the same unacceptable by the seekers of truth. The attitude is further unreasonable as the writers of the Four Canonical Gospels have not claimed their Gospels to have been written under inspiration — how can such writings be set as criterion for judging the book that was written under inspiration. There is, however, no doubt about the fact that to discover the fact that to discover the reality about the Gospel of St. Barnabas and its authenticity is an extremely difficult task. The Christian Historians and research scholars have exerted their best efforts to know when and in which language it was first written, but they appear to have failed to come to certain definite conclusions.

Although, it is not difficult to trace the authenticity of St. Barnabas' Gospel with regard to when, where and in which language it was written, the two general Epistles of St. Barnabas help a great deal in this behalf. In their light it can be determined that the Gospel of St. Barnabas was written in C. 131, and was translated into Italian language. This oldest, well-known and trustworthy Italian version is safe in the Imperial Library of Vienna, the Capital of Austria. From amongst the persons, whose names cannot be effaced, from the pages of history. Mr. Cramer, Counsellor to the King of Prussia, was the first to get this Italian version in 1709 C.E. while he was in Amsterdam (Holland). After four years i.e. 1713, he presented it to Prince Eugene of Savoy who in 1738 transferred it along with his library to Vienna, where it still avails the truth seekers.

The only oldest copy of the Gospel of St. Barnabas which claims worldwide fame and that has been translated in English, Arabic and Urdu languages, is in the Italian language and is safely preserved in the Royal Library of Vienna. It contains 220 leaves of thick paper, bound by thin but stiff boards covered with a leather surface of a dark bronze-green colour, simply ornamented with a double gift line close to the edge (the inner line avoiding the corners, so as to form a sort of triangle), with a floreated centre-piece embossed without gilding or colour, but fringed by a double gilded border line somewhat arabesque in character. This binding is generally regarded as of Asian origin, there is, however, a small group which regards it to be the work of the two Parisian binders whom the Duke of Paris had employed to bind this book which was then in his possession.

It is also said that a particular agreement in Venice has a similar binding, so that not the slightest difference can be pointed out. This striking similarity sets one to beleive that both must have been the handi-work of the same artist. In short, the binding does not in the least help one decide about the time the Gospel of Barnabas was written. Binding of a book may take place at any time and thus it is not reasonable to judge the time a book was written in relation with the time it was bound.

Paper

Christian Apologetics say that the paper used for the Gospel of St. Barnabas is of Turkish origin, but this opinion does not hold firm when we check the paper carefully, as all leaves of the book are of a paper known as — Italian Paper. It is a durable but rough paper. Only two of its pages are smoothened and glazed which are remarkably distinct from the rest of the leaves on account of their colour. But the inner side of the paper used in this Gospel contains such marks which are not characteristic of any of the Asian or Turkish papers. The water marks of this paper depict an anchor inside a circle. According to reputed scholars the said marks are the characteristic of the Italian paper.

Date of Binding:

Among those personalities whose names have not been erased by History is Mr. J . F. Cramer, counselor to the King of Prussia, who was the first to find the Italian version of the Gospel of Barnabas. He was in Amsterdam (Holland) when he came across the copy of the Gospel of St. Barnabas, He found it in the library of a famous citizen of the said city, and he mentioned the owner of the book in undistinct terms and said that the owner regarded the book as most valuable. After four years, however, Mr. Cramer presented the book to Prince Eugene of Savoy. The said prince, despite his pre-occupation with wars and politics, was also interested in arts and the relics of history. In 1738 he submitted this book together with his entire Library to the Court of Vienna, where it is preserved up to this day.

Here, we want to put forward the point that the binding of the Gospel of St. Barnabas must have taken place when the book, together with the Library of the said Prince, was being transferred to the Royal Library. Experience proves that binding may take place at any time after the writing of a book hence, to date a book with the period that corresponds to that of the binding is quite unreasonable.

The authenticity of the Gospel of St. Barnabas cannot be denied by pointing out the quality of paper, the binding of the book or style of narration, for the same measuring stick can also be applied to the Four Cononical Gospels. For example:

"The writer of the Gospel according to John was one of those who set out to take advantage of the opportunity. Who John was, we do not know for certain. He may have been the John; son of Zabedee who comes into the story of the first three Gospels (though he is never mentioned by name in the fourth). If so, he must have been a very old man when he wrote the Gospel, and indeed, tradition says that he lived to a great age. Some think it was written by another John called the "elder"of whom we know nothing, or indeed by some quite unknown person. In any case, it is

very generally agreed that it was written at Ephesus, about
A.D. 100 —, perhaps a little earlier, perhaps a little later.

With regard to the Gospel of Matthew, Dummelow
says, "Direct authorship of this Gospel by Matthew is
improbable".[18] As. regards Mark, he says, "internal evidence points definitely to the conclusions that the last twelve
verses i.e. 16:9—20 are not by St. Mark.[19] The explanation
as to how these verses found a place here is very interesting.
It is stated that the Gospel of Mark, being the first authoritative account of the life of Jesus, gained a good circulatior
at first, but, later on .Matthew and Luke became more
popular, and Mark was, to say, put in shade. When at the
close of the apostelic age an attempt was made (probably
in Rome) to collect the authentic memorials of the
Apostles and their companions, a copy of the neglected
second Gospel was not easily found. The one that was
actually discovered and was used to multiply copies, had lost
some leaves, and so a fitting termination (this present
Appendix) was added by "another hand"[20]

Further, commenting on the well known confession of
Jesus, "Why callest thou me good"(Mark 10:17) Dummelow
says that in the revised version of Mathew, Cirist's reply is,
"Why askest thou me concerning that which is good" and
adds: The author of Mathew altered the text slightly, to prevent the readers from supposing that Christ denied that he
was good."[21]

In addition to the proof which is furnished by the
Church History and by Dummelow's Bible commentary, indi-
cates that there is a contradiction and absurdity of the
Four canonical Gospels. In Chain Reference Bible is recorded
that "all the original manuscripts of the Bible have
perished.[22]

---

18. See, a *History of the Christian Church.* pp. 42; 62 by Prof.
Milliston Walker of Ecclesiastical History in Yale University. See
also Unger's Bible and Books by Merrill F. Unger p. 884.

19. *Critical Introduction of the Gospel of Barnabas* by Mr. and Mrs.
Ragg.

20. *Bible Commentary* by Dummelow p. 733.

21. *Ibid.,* .p. 730.

22 *Chain Reference Bible,* p. 180.

It may be said that Jesus was the "SUN OF RIGHTEOUS-NESS" and hence the language and the metaphors; but there are certain reported utterances of Jesus which do not admit of such explanation. "And no man hath ascended up to heaven, save the son of man, who is in heaven." Jesus as a jew, did believe that at least two men, Enoch and Elijah, had ascended into heaven, and therefore he could not say that not say that no man has ascended into heaven. Jesus at the time of this utterance does not befit the real Jesus; he was on the earth, but accords well enough with the SUN-GOD who comes down from heaven at his birth, and ascends into heaven again, and yet remains all the time in heaven

The Spanish Version

Moreover, there was found a Spanish version of the Gospel of Barnabas in the early 18th Century. It consisted of 221 chapters and 223 parts, and the pages numbered 420. It was, however, lost in the course of time. It was taken by the famous orientalist "Sell from Dr. Hemett of Hedley in Hampshire. The book next came into the possession of Dr. Monk-house who was a member of Queens College of Oxford University. He translated it into English and later no, in 1874, he presented the translation together with the Spanish version to the former Professor Dr. White.

Dr. White mentioned this book and quoted some of its passages in one of his lectures which he particularly prepared for his students. When the translation of the Spanish version was compared with the Italian version, it agreed remarkable, as it was directly translated from the Italian version which was preserved in the Royal Library of Vienna. I did not find any difference with the exception of two points: Italian version says "When the treacherous Judas came with a band of Roman soldiers, to surrender Jesus to them, he was close to the room where his disciples slept. When Jesus heard tramping of the Roman soldiers, he was afraid and entered in the said room. God notices the danger to the surrounded Jesus and sent four of His angles who carried Jesus through an opening near the ceiling to the third heaven. When the treacherous Judas entered the room, his facial features and voice were miraculously turned into those of Jesus. Meanwhile the disciples woke up and saw him, they believed that he was Jesus himself."

The Spanish version agrees with the Italian version except that it adds "except Peter which means that it does not describe Peter as one of those disciples who entertained not the slightest doubt about Judas being Jesus. It further mentions the name of one of the angels who carried Jesus as "Israel" while the Italian version mentions the name as "Oureal". There are also a few differences of trifling nature which we leave over.

The Story of Monk

Sell has given a side note on his translation of the Spanish Version saying that the early part of it suggests it to be a translation from the Italian version and that the person who translated it was an Arrogonian Muslim named Mustafa de Aranda. Besides, in the preface, the translation has given the annecdote of the discoverer of the Gospel. He was an Italian Monk, Fra-Marino. It says that Fra-Marino somehow came across a number of articles of Irenaens and that one of these articles revealed the truth about "Paul". This article was written by Irenaens quoting from the Gospel of Barnabas from authority. Fra-Marino was therefore interested to find the Gospel of Barnabas. By a fortunate stroke of chance Fra-Marino became the favourite of Pope Sixtus V for some time, as such he once had the opportunity of visiting the Library of the Pope together with him. As luck would have it, the Pope felt drowsy and slept, and in the meanwhile Fra-Marino intended to read certain book to pass the time. The first book he came across was his long sought for treasure, the Gospel of St. Barnabas. Availing himself of the opportunity he hid the book in his clothes, and when the Pope woke up, he took permission and came out with his treasure. Later on he embraced Islam after studying the Gospel.

The story of Monk Fra-Marino is recorded in the preface of Spanish version, and so has "Sell" quoted it in the preface of his translation. So, this story and the passages quoted by Professor White in his lectures are the only two sources of the Gospel of St. Barnabas. It, however, disappeared and nothing is known about how it came to be lost. The last report about it was that it was given to Dr. Monk-House for translation and that the said gentleman submitted both the original book and the translation to Dr. Hewett. Thereafter, all traces of it were lost to posterity.

Observation

Here, there arises a question whether the copy of Italian version stolen by Monk Fra Marino from the library of Pope Sixtus V and that which is preserved in the Royal Library of Vienna are one and the same or two different versions? If both are one and the same, which of them is the first and which was transcribed after it. These questions cannot be rightly answered until it is known when the original version was written. Neither the knowledge about the period of Pope Sixtus V nor the quality of the Italian paper can give the clue relating to which of the two is the original one — that which is in the Royal Library of Vienna or that which was stolen by Monk Fra Marino.

The fame of the Gospel of St. Barnabas spread in the early 18th Century and it set a thrill throughout the religious and educated circles of Europe. England was particularly the most interested of all European countries in this matter. The learned discussions of scholars gradually assumed the form of wilful and whimsical thought based on unreasonable assumptions. The most important point of their discussion was whether the Italian version of the Gospel of St. Barnabas was the original one which was stolen by Fra Marino from the Pope's Library or which was copied from yet another book.

Arabic Note on the Margin

When a rational thinker finds Arabic note on the margins of an Italian Gospel, he is struck by wonder but he will by no means admit

(a) That notes on the margin constitute a part of the original Gospel, i.e. the Author has written the points he forgot to mention in the main Gospel on the margins in a language other than that of the said Gospel

(b) Careful study reveals that the notes on the margin are

written in a sound style in certain places, though the transcriber has spoilt it to a great extent by wrong spelling, wrong
construction and improper substitution of words, so much...
so that no side can be extracted from it without great
effort and concentration. The construction is so vague that
it is difficult to understand whether the transcriber has
written the original word or has given its explanation

(c) The language of the notes is of a high and beautiful style
in certain places while in other places it appears to be non-
Arabic style. It is quite clear that one who can write a high
flown language cannot make such errors which cannot be
expected even from an orientalist. It is, therefore, reasonable to conclude that the writers of the notes on the margins
are more than one person. The first of them wrote most
beautifully while the next of them spoilt his writing. I mean
to say that the Arabic notes on the margins of the copy
preserved in the Royal Library of Vienna does not prove that
the writer of the Italian version of the Gospel was an Arab
Muslim. It has never been seen that an author writes his
book in one language (Italian) and writes his notes on the
margin in another language (Arabic). Much less can it
determine the date of writing it.

If we admit that the book stolen by Fra-Marino from
the Pope's library and that which is in the Royal Library
of Vienna are copies of one and the same version, the
question arises that which of them was the first and original?
It is extremely difficult to answer this question. What we
have said about the Arabic notes on the margins proves that
the writer of these notes was neither an Arab nor a Muslim.
It is the notes of a person who had happened to read the
book. It may, however, be guessed that the writer of the
notes was either a Tascanian or Vanitian, but not the Monk-
Fra-Marino, who stole the Gospel from the Pope's Library.
It could have been regarded as the work of the Monk, had
it been the same copy that was stolen by him. Hence
opinions of Laura and Lonsdale Ragg are baseless and un-
sound. Whatever the case is, we can at least be sure that
the writer of the Gospel of St. Barnabas was a person who
was fully conversant with the Latin Old Testament, and that
he was aware of the Christian Script much more than the

Islamic Literature. It is, therefore, probable that it was Barnabas, as he alone possessed the said qualification among the disciples of Jesus.

Dante

Christian Apologists regard the writer of St. Barnabas as a person who lived after Dante as the description of Heaven and Hell in Barnabas similar (agrees) with the description of Dante. Drs. Jan Slomps also hold the opinion that the writer of Barnabas was either a contemporary of Dante or lived after him, and that the ideas presented by St. Barnabas were peculiar to that particular time. So, from this point of view, the writer of Barnabas proves to be a person living in the 14th Century A.D. But as a matter of fact the agreement between the description of Dante and Barnabas may also be a mere coincidence. The right opinion in this respect would be that is that the source of this similarity of expression must be something is older than both, in which case it will not be necessary to regard the two as contemporaries. The said ancient source may be regarded as the ancient Greek mythology. Hence, in this light, it will be improper to base the similarity of expression on mere coincidence.

Persian Empire B.C. 536—330

History bears witness to the fact that the Israelites did not enjoy the liberty of reading, writing and speaking the Hebrew language during their period of captivity by the Iranians. When the King Cyrus emancipated them from the bondage, Ezra rewrote the Old Testament and reconstructed the Temple. During the period of captivity the concept of Satan as prevailed among the Iranians entered into the Jewish religion. It is, then, reasonable to regard the similarity between the concept of Satan among the Jews and among the Iranians as coincidence? Your reply in this respect will also be the reply irrespect with the similarity of expressions between Dante and Barnabas.

Arabic Version.

Christian Apologists tend to think that the Italian

version of the Gospel of St. Barnabas is a translation from its Arabic version. This opinion was first expressed by Cramer in his introduction when he presented the Italian version to Prince Eugene — he wrote that it was a compilation of certain Muhammadan and translated into Italian from Arabic or some other language. Following Cramer in his opinion, *la Mote* says:" a Baron Homindrof, a noble, cultured and widely informed person, showed me a book which the Turks regard as the Holy Gospel of Barnabas, but it is obviously translated into Italian from Arabic". By the term "Turks" La Mote means Muslims in general or Arabs, whom many of the European writers have termed in general as Turks.

Later on, Dr. White, who has earlier been mentioned, said in 1784 that the original Arabic text still existed in Asia. After deeper consideration, it will be realised that the statement of Dr. White, is based on the writing of Sell which were published about fifty years earlier, in which Sell terms his statements as 'introductory' discussions. In the same discussions he says:

"The Muslims have an Arabic Gospel which they name as St. Barnabas's Gospel. It contains the biography of Jesus in quite a different way than the four Canonical Gospels, and agrees with what Muhammad (p.b.u.h.) wrote in his Quran."[2] [3]

After writing these words, he admits that he never had the opportunity to see the Gospel of Barnabas, which proves that his ideas were based on stray reports, and that he follows the opinion of *La Mote* who in turn bases his opinion on stray reports, as he too had never seen the Gospel of Barnabas.

It is, however, strange to note the Muslim Historians and Chronicle writers, both ancient and contemporary, have remained silent about the Gospel of St. Barnabas as if they have never heard of it. It is still strange to note that even those scholars whose sole occupation is to debate on religion seem to be totally unaware of the said Gospel, despite the

---

23. *Introduction of the Gospel of Barnabas* under discussion by Rev. Ragg.

fact that it could have proved as effective in proving their stand as a drawn sword. Even the Bibliographers, the Arabs, the non-Arabs and the Orientalists, who have devoted themselves to prepare exhaustive lists of books, both old and new, have made no mention of the Gospel of Barnabas. It seems unbelievable that they would have ignored to mention it even if they had only heard of it.

Christian Apologists tend to believe that the Gospel of St. Barnabas first appeared in the early medieval centuries in the Italian languages, and that the writer of the Gospel also belonged to the same period. They support their opinion by saying that the Gospel contains the songs sung by peasants while harvesting as are still sung in the Tascanian countries including Italy. The Gospel further mentions the carving of stones and the erection of stony structures which suggests that the author was the inhabitant of a country where this art was practised, else how can an inhabitant of tents in deserts imagine these arts. The Gospel of St .Barnabas also contains the description of how the slaves carry the meals of workers of their masters who worked in the Vine-Yards, the squeezing of grapes by feet and distillation of wine etc., which cannot be imagined by an Arab. The truth is that the Gospel of St. Barnabas are nowhere to be found in Arabia, though in Syria and Palestine these conditions are still to be found. Right from the time of Jesus upto this time, the farmers still sing their rustic songs at the time of harvest, while the masons and the carvers of the stone still work in the same way as mentioned by St. Barnabas. In syria and Palestine, there still live the labourers working in the Vine-Yards of their masters. This proves that the Gospel of St. Barnabas was written at the time of Apostolic Age.

The writer of the Gospel of St. Barnabas was jew who had followed Jesus, and he was undoubtedly a disciple of Jesus. It is most unfortunate that the Spanish version of the Gospel is lost, and still more regrettable is the fact that the Scholars who had the chance of seeing it, failed to study it in a scholarly manner. Further it is also unfortunate that we

have no detailed information about Mustafa, the Person who
translated it into Spanish, for it would have been most
interesting to know of a person who had acquired skill in
both Italian and Spanish languages with which the Gospel
of Barnabas is related.

The Greek Version

Mr. & Mrs. Ragg has mentioned in their critical
Introduction of the Gospel of Barnabas, but they did not
discuss the matter in detail. It, however, proves that the
Epistles of Barnabas were read in many of the Churches
during the early Christian Era. The Gospel of Barnabas
also appeared during the same period. However, when the
Trinitarians came to power, the Epistles and Gospel of
Barnabas were destroyed.

Ragg in his introduction on page 46, writes under the
items possibly drawn from Gnostic Barnabas: "First, the
solitary fragment of the original Barnabas that remains to
us" — then he quotes a verse in the Greek, which gives the
idea that even like the Italian and Spanish versions "there
was also a Greek version of the Gospel of Barnabas, which
is now lost, except for a few fragments".

The Jubilee Year

Christian Apologists say that the Gospel of Barnabas
contains a particular statement which decides the time
of its compilation. The said statement sets the Jubilee once
in every hundred years, though the Jews celebrated a Jubilee
every fifty years.[23a] The Jubilee is nowhere mentioned in
the History except in relation with the Roman Church as
celebrating the Jubilee at the end of a century. The Jubilee
was celebrated for the first time by Pope Boniface VIII
decreed in 1300 C.E. and he decreed that it should be celebrated at the opening of every new century. But since the
celebration of the Jubilee had filled the treasures of the
Pope, it was decided by Pope Clement VI could not wait till
1400 but decided in 1343 to reduce the period to fifty

23a. *Leviticus* 25:8—55 and 27: 16—25.

years. Pope Paul II (1464–1471), again reduced the period to Twenty five years.[24]

Dr. Khalil Sadaat (Christian) of Egypt writes that the statement of Barnabas relating to the Jubilee as being held once in every century sets the period of its compilation as the first half. of the 14th century. But when we take into consideration the vast information of the compiler of the Gospel of St. Barnabas relating to the journeys of the ancient period, it seems difficult to believe that such a scholar would make such an error as to 'set the period of Jubilee as once in a century. Such error is not possible even from a layman. It may, therefore, be considered that the error was made by the transcriber who read 'hundred' and wrote it by mistake while transcribing from yet another book, as the spelling of hundred and fifty is so striking similar that one may easily make a mistake in reading.[25]

Further, more than half of the Gospel of Barnabas agrees with the sources of the Four Gospels and the Old Testament. It mentions the climate of Palestine, agriculture, rivers and social life which proves that it was compiled during the period of Jesus. History records that the Nicean Council and the decrees of Popes brand a number of books as forbidden, including the Gospel of Barnabas. It proves that the said Gospel existed long before the birth of the Holy Prophet (p.b.u.h.).

Drs. Jan Slomps and Christian Apologists write that the Gospel of St. Barnabas differs from the Holy Qur'an. If it is so, he should have believed it as the Four Gospels also differ from the Holy Quran. This difference between the Holy Quran and the Gospel of Barnabas proves that neither was it written by a Muslim nor was it written during the time of the Holy Quran. The "Gospel" which the Holy Quran recognises is one single Gospel and not the Four Gospels Matthew, Mark, Luke and John the Pseudo-writers.

Referring to the objections raised by Christian Apologists against the present Gospel of St. Barnabas, I can say those and more can truly and safely be applied to all those Four Gospels. The story of the present Gospel of

---

24. *Encyclopaedia Britannica*, Vol. 13, page 100.
25. *Introduction of the Arabic Gospel of St. Barnabas.*

St. Barnabas alleged to be the work of other than Barnabas, has not so far been authentically repudiated by bringing forward the real and original Gospel of St. Barnabas or any other Counter Gospel of St. Barnabas in Aramaic language and unless such a book is produced, examined and scrutinized minutely, there cannot be any convincing reason to challenge the validity and authenticity of the present Gospel of St. Barnabas though many many objections and explanations may be put forward. The present Gospel of St. Barnabas alleged to be in Italian and found by Fra-Marino is said to be translation of the original Gospel of St. Barnabas — where this original? The Christians who thoroughly know the evolutionary history of the Four Gospels do know that all of them were compiled, long after the death of Jesus; that no conclusive proof has been put forward that those are the real teachings of Jesus especially when contradictions etc. are found there is abundance. There is no doubt that those Gospels were compiled in democratic methods of Greeks, they cannot therefore be the real words and sayings of Jesus for his language was Aramaic, and all of the Gospels are in Greek, which is Greek to him.

To sum up I say that St. Barnabas was without doubt admittedly one of the ordained disciples of Jesus, who saw Jesus, touched him, remained in his company, sat with him, heard his sermons, wrote down his teachings under his directions. Further, he did produce a Gospel based on words, sayings and teachings of Jesus.

Dr. Khalil Bek Saadat of Egypt, a Christian Scholar, writes: the author of the Gospel of Barnabas was a theologian of a high status, a man of great literary skill and capable of presenting his arguments with great skill in support of his stand. But he crossed the reasonable limits in this respect until he spoilt the desired effect, had avoided the mention of Holy Prophet Muhammad's name and contented himself with the prophecies"

....

"Over and above these qualities, the Gospel contains wisdom, philosophy, moral teachings, beautiful literary style and rhetoric expression which put together proves most attractive. The easy-flow of the expression is extremely interesting. The Gospel is a good effort at raising noble human feelings to a great height, purifying man of baser animal feelings. It forbids evil and encourages virtue and induces man to serve humanity. It advocates self-sacrifice, devotion to God and service to mankind".

The statement of Dr. Khalil Saadat, makes it clear that the name of the Holy Prophet was clearly mentioned in the Gospel of St. Barnabas. The rejection of the Gospel is in fact based on the dislike of the Holy Prophet, though the Four Gospels also contain the· mention of the Holy Prophet indirectly.

Had the FOUR GOSPELS contained a statement of Jesus saying that there would be no Prophet after him, it could have been said that the Gospel of St. Barnabas differed from the four Gospels. But as a matter of fact Jesus never claimed to be the last Prophet as proved by the four Gospels.

On the contrary Jesus said,

"And I will pray the Father, and he shall give you another comforter, that he may abide with you for ever". (John 14:16).

"But the comforter, which is the Holy Ghost, whom the Father will send in my name, he shall teach you all things, and bring all things to your remembrance, whatsoever I have said unto you". (John 14:26).

The above verses clearly indicate that the message of Jesus was not the final and perfect and that someone else will perfect Jesus' message. We are not bound by the impression of those who are followers of Jesus. There is enough material in the sayings of Jesus himself that enables us to conclude that he was one of the PROPHETS OF GOD, that he never claimed any kind of God-head for himself, and that he did not come into the world to act as a scapegoat for other's sins.

It is, however, true that much foreign matter derived

from Paganism was incorporated in the teachings of Jesus. Things never taught by him are passed off under his name.

Jesus could not reveal the whole truth. He had many things to say unto his disciples, but they were unable to bear them. He, however, gave them the good news of another great Prophet coming after him, the spirit of truth, for he says, "Will guide you into all truth; for he will show you things to come." Muhammad (s.a.w.) came and taught Islam in its perfect form, and that was the religion of Jesus.

(4)

THE AUTHENTICITY OF
THE GOSPEL OF BARNABAS

To begin with, we shall examine the following quotations:

(1) "The earliest designationof a passage from the Gospels as "Scripture" was about C131, by the so-called Barnabas[26] and of quotation from Paul about C110—117, by Polycorp.[27] By the time of Justin (c-153), the Gospels were read in the services in Rome, together with Old Testament Prophets.[28] The Process by which the New Testament writings came to scriptural authority seems to have one of anology. The Old Testament was everywhere regarded as divinely authoritative. Christians could think no less of their own fundamental books. The question was an open one, however, as to which were the canonical writings. Works like Hermas and Barnabas were read in churches. An authoritative list was desirable. Marcion had prepared such a canon for his followers.[29]

(2) "The author who wrote the name of Barnabas, possibly in Alexandria"(c. 131).[30]

(3) "There was clearly a great deal of writing by Christians in the period. from say A.D. 60 to 160. In addition to our New Testament books they read in the Churches. These were first the Epistle of Barnabas.[31]

Mr. Bashir Mahmood M.A., writes in his introduction to the Urdu version of the Gospel of St. Barnabas, as follows, which, we hope, will interest our readers.

---

26. Barn. 4
27. Phil. 12
28. Apology, 66, 67.
29. *A History of the Christian Church* by Williston Walker, Prof. of Ecciesiastical in Yale University, pp. 62.
30. *Ibid.*, pp. 42.
31. *An Outline of Church History.* by the Rev. C.H. Dodd, D.D.,pp.68

(4) "Lightfoot, a research scholar of Liverpool, quoted from Encyclopaedia of Britannica,[32] that the Gospel of Barnabas was written between C 69 and C 79 during the reign of the Roman Emperor Vespasian".

These quotations show that the Gospel of St. Barnabas existed in the early churches as a canonical Gospel and was read in church service. But alas: when the non jews joined the Church, they transformed Jesus into one of their mythological gods. The importance of the Gospel of St. Barnabas ended after the council of Nicaea 325 CE. Had this Gospel been canonised in the Nicena council, the road to Mecca would have been open to all Christians and the Church would have consequently been abdicated. Beside blocking the Road to Mecca, there is not a single reason to ignore of this Gospel.

So far as the Divine purpose of the Bible is concerned, it was meant for and confined to a "tribe". As such its scope of guidance was limited to such an extent that even the conception of God was tribal. God was not "God of the Worlds" but was known as God of Abraham and God of Jacob. And thus Jesus had to come, to seek the "Lost Sheep of Israel."

Now, in the light of the Gospel of St. Barnabas, it is for Christianity in general to see whether it should still cling to the uncertian and obsolete "tribal" belief or to become an integral part of the great fraternity of Islam and help make the world free from destructive conflicts.

It is, however, true that much foreign matter derived from Paganism was incorporated in the religion of Jesus. Things never taught by him are passed off under his name. He never claimed to be God or the son of God. If Jesus, for the sake of argument, was neither God nor son of the God, in the sense in which the Church accepts him, would it not be injurious to his memory to worship him as God? It is not love, but a sort of infatuation to bring him under an unintentional libel. It is a disgrace, and not an honour, to call any person a son of a King, when he is not. We shall describe this point with some detail in the following chapters

32. *Encyclopaedia Britannica*, Vol. 3, p. 118.

The oldest and the most famous copy of the Gospel of St. Barnabas is not in its own Hebrew language in which it should have been written, but is in Italian language which was never his language, and that is safely deposited in the Prince's Library, Vienna.

There was, however, found a Spanish version of the Gospel of St. Barnabas in the eighteenth century which was translated into English by Dr. Monkhouse, Fellow of Queen's College, Oxford, and which is now lost. Dr. White writes that the translation made by Dr. Monkhouse agreed word by word with the Italian version of the Gospel of Barnabas, with no difference worth mentioning, except in the order.

The notes made by Sale on the Spanish version are expressive of the fact that it was a translation from the Italian version, made by an Arragonian Muslim named MUSTAFA' We however, have no further information about him, though it would have been most interesting to know about a Muslim who had a firm grip over both Italian and Spanish languages. These are the only languages through which the Gospel of St. Barnabas became known to the world. It is regrettable that the Church neglected to record the bio-data of such a benefactor.

The Spanish version of the Gospel contains in its preface the interesting anecdote of a Christian Monk, called Fra-Marino, who acquired the version of the said Gospel from the Library of Pope Sextus V, and finally embraced Islam. The anecdote has been recorded by Sell in his translation of the Holy Quran. This anecdote and the quotations from the lectures of Dr. White give us an idea about the Spanish version of the Gospel of St. Barnabas, but nothing is known about how it was lost. It is, however known that the translation and the real Spanish version were both handed over to Dr. White by Dr. Monkhouse and no further information could be had of it thereafter.

There arises a question here, i.e. whether the said version which Monk Fra-Marino had obtained from the Library of Pope Sextus V and the one that is kept in the Prince's Library, Vienna, are one and the same? If they are different, it must then be admitted that the latter is not the real Spanish version which the Monk Fra-Marino had obtained from the Library of the Pope, and that the one at Vienna is the translation or transcription from certain other copy of the Gospel, and it is not right to regard it as the first and the original version. Since the language of St. Barnabas was Aramaic, even as that of his Master Jesus, it is probable that he wrote the Gospel in the Aramaic Language, from which the present translation was made.

Ragg(Introduction, page 46) writes under the title "Items possibly drawn from Gnostic Barnabas, First, the solitary fragment of the original Barnabas that remains to us", — then he quotes a verse in the Greek, which gives the idea that even like the Italian and Spanish versions, "There was also a greek version of the Gospel of St. Barnabas, which is now lost, except for a few fragments."

When Barnabas' relics was discovered in a tomb at Cyprus in the fourth year of Emperor Zeno, a copy of the Gospel was found lying on his breast. Here, there arose certain questions of great importance, i.e., in which language was it written? Was it in the Italian language? Was it a transcription from yet another copy? Was it the same copy which Monk Fra-Marino had obtained from the Pope's library? Or was it of a totally different nature? And how was the Gospel buried with Barnabas, and where is this Gospel now?

The Gospel of St. Barnabas which was published by Oxford contains Arabic writings on its margins, which sets one wondering. It seems worth while to discuss this matter with some detail.

The language of these notes on the margins seem to be sound, though it has been spoilt by the transcriber; at places there is wrong spelling and at others the words have been tampered with and at still other places the expressions are totally unintelligible despite every effort to decipher at certain places, possessive phrases which have been used in wrong order. This clearly shows that it was not written by any Arab.

After a deeper study of these notes one finds that the language used in them is sound and beautiful Arabic basically, which suggests that their writer possessed a sound knowledge of Arabic. The mistakes of spelling and language that are found here and there suggest that either the margins were written by different persons or that they were trans-scribed by a person who was not well versed in Arabic and has, therefore, rendered the expression unintelligible at places. What I meant by this discussion is to say that the Italian version of the Gospel of St. Barnabas that is in the Prince's Library, Vienna, is undoubtedly a transcription from yet another copy of the same, and that it is not right to believe it to be the first and original version. After admitting that the Italian version of Vienna is not original Gospel which the Monk Fra-Marino had taken or stolen from the Pope's Library, there arises the question about the original Gospel from which the present copy of Vienna has been transcribed.

Further, the use of the possessive phrases in wrong order suggest most clearly that the original Gospel from which it was transcribed was either old Latin or Italian. The same opinion has been expressed by trusted scholars about the Italian version at the Vienna Library. The experts in calligraphy have expressed the view that it must have been written by certain Venetian during the Sixteenth century or early seventeenth century. It is most probable that the original book from which this copy was transcribed was either Tascanian or Venetican, though the Tascanian Phrases have found their way in it. These are the statements of Lonsdale and Loura Ragg who have based them on the views of Italian Scholars.

The Arabic notes on the margins of the Gospel of St. Barnabas do not prove its compiler to be a Muslim Arab, as a careful study of the Gospel reveals that its compiler was a thorough scholar of the Old Testament who was not only well versed in matter of religions but was also well acquainted with the day to day life of the people who lived at the time of Jesus. A dweller of the sandy deserts of Arabia could very well imagine of places, but he could not picture to himself how wine is extracted from grapes and how people work in farms. It is known only to a Palestinean. It is regrettable that the Greek, the Aramaic and the Spanish versions of the Gospel of Barnabas are lost; it is further more regrettable that those of the scholars who had these versions did not make scholarly research about them as they did with the Italian version. It is regrettable that the Christian scholars have claimed that the compiler of the Gospel of Barnabas was a contemporary of Dante the Poet, only because he mentions the Hell and the Satan. Did not Zoroaster mention Hell and Satan? If so, does it prove that the writers of the Four Gospels have had inspiration from Zoroaster? Yet another argument against the Gospel of Barnabas is presented by saying that he mentioned the jubilee to be held once in a century, and that it was so at the time of Dante. But Dr. Khalil Saadat, an Egyptian Christian Scholar, says that, "when we compare this error with the vast information of the Old Testament which Barnabas had, we can easily conclude that a scholar of his rank could not commit such an error, that it must have been the error of the transcriber. This idea is further strengthened by the fact that there exists only slight difference between the figures fifty and hundred in the Italian language and that a slight error in transcription can make figure fifty seem like hundred."

To say that the Gospel of Barnabas was compiled during the medieval centuries is the outcome of a mind that is given to wander away from the right path, as most of this Gospel is based on the material that is contained in the Teaching of the Prophets of the O.T. It also contains certain detailed narrations which are mentioned briefly in three (Synoptic) Gospels of the Carfels, as it was originally delivered in C.131 for catechetical instruction.[33] The Christians should have received and welcomed it with open heart, but, alas! prejudice prompted them to declare this Divine Writ incredulous.

In 492 C.E. the Pope Gelasius, issued decree branding a number of books as unfit for reading and the Gospel of Barnabas was one of the prohibited books. It was long before the birth of the Holy Prophet, which is a proof of the fact that the Gospel had not upto that time assumed its present form, as its reading was prohibited by the Pope. If the book had been out of the reach of common folk, it must have surely been known to scholars, and in such case the Holy Prophet would have surely heard about it, more particulary because it contains the name of the Holy Prophet most clearly. He was the founder of a great movement,

---

33. See *Introduction of the urdu Branabas*, printed in Bombay, p.15.

enlivened his dead nation to the amazement of the world at large and was famed throughout the world, for his great achievements, Yet it is amazing that neither he nor his early successors ever heard the name of the Gospel of St. Barnabas; even the Arabs who conquered Spain knew nothing about it. It is regrettable to note that the condemnation of the Gospel of St. Barnabas by the Pope is now considered as a false report; if it were false, is the burning of the books also a false report. (See Encyclopaedia Britannica).

The authenticity of the Gospel of Barnabas is most evident, but the sick hearts that are given to finding faults shall always remain deprived of the appreciation of truth. They have eyes but they see not, they have ears but they hear not, they have hearts but they feel not and they have minds but they think not. The teachings of the Gospel of Barnabas are themselves the greatest proof of its authenticity, that enlighten the heart and incline it towards purity. Further, history itself bears witness that it makes one feel as if one is being spoken to by God Himself.

Dr. Khalil Bek Saadat of Egypt, a Christian Scholar, writes in his introduction of the Arabic version of the Gospel of Barnabas, "The points in which the Gospel of Barnabas differ from the recognized Four Gospels, are as follows":

1. Barnabas says that "Jesus denied his Divineship and also denied his being the Son of God."

2. "That the Son whom Abraham intended to sacrifice was Ismail"

3. "That Jesus did not die on the cross".

4. "And that the Promised Messiah was not Jesus, it was the Holy Prophet Muhammad"

"Barnabas has mentioned the name of the Holy Prophet in clear terms and mentioned him as the Prophet of God.'" He further said that "when Adam was expelled from the heaven he found, "there is no God but Allah and Muhammad is the Messenger of Allah", written on the gate of heaven in words of light".[34]

There is no doubt about the fact that the author of the Gospel of Barnabas was endowed with a divinity style of writing and had fully command of expression. He was an expert in argumentation and could present evidences to prove his claim most skilfully. Yet, in this respect, he has gone far beyond the necessary hints and it may be seen, extremism spoils the game. If only Barnabas had made secret hints towards the Holy Prophet suggestive of his being the promised Prophet, he would have served the purpose and would not have needed to mention his name clearly with lengthy explanation. If he had confined himself to writing the two Articles of Faith alone as having been seen by Adam on the Gate of heaven, his purpose would have been served most satisfactorily".

The quotation given above clearly shows that the real motive behind the denial of the Gospel of Barnabas is their hsotility to the Holy Prophet and the rest are mere pretensions. In the following pages we shall prove the claim of Barnabas from the Four Recognized Gospels Insha Allah.

Generally, the Gospel of Barnabas is termed as the Muhammadan Gospel, but it is strange to note that no Muslim historian has ever mentioned the said Gospel. Even the religious scholars who debated over religious matters make no mention of it though it would have served their prupose most decisively. Further, all catalogues of the Arab and non-Arab scholars of Islam are free from the mention of this book, even like the catalogues of the orientalists which contain the name of the rare books that were prepared after great search and labour. If it had been known publicly, they would certainly have come by it and made a mention of it in their catalogues. This is a further proof of the fact that Gospel of Barnabas was altogether unknown to Muslims.

Any way, even as Martin Luther had emancipated the Bible from the prison of the Pope; Fra-Marino was chosen by God to emancipate the Gospel of St. Barnabas from the prison of yet another Pope. This reminds us of how God planned the emancipation of Israel from the clutches of

---

34. Taken from *Introduction to Barnabas* by Rev. Ragg under discussion.

Pharaoh by bringing Moses in the Palace of tyrant for His own glory. Strange are the actions of God whose wisdom no man can fanthom.[34a]

In the Encyclopaedia, under the heading "Apocryphal Literature" is an entry.

"Gospel of Barnabas condemned in the Gelasian Decree. Decretune Gelasianum is described as a compilation of documents anterior to St. Gregory (C .540—C. 604) and it is difficult to determine Gelasius" contribution to it, and at all events as we know it, it is of Roman origin and sixth century or later." Gelasius is explained as Gelasius, St., confirmed the estrangement between the eastern and western churches by insisting on the removal of the name of Acacius, Bishop of Constantinople, from the deptychs."

In the first place, if the Gelasian Decree is anterior to St. Gregory, who died at 604 C.E. March 12th[34b] then it cannot be 'later' than the sixth century except by a maximum of four or five years. In any case, it would be anterior to Islam, which was not born till 623 C.E., much later than even circa 604. In addition, if the Gospel of St. Barnabas was "condemned in the Gelasian Decree", then how can a document which had been condemned before Islam was born, be forged by a Muslim convert nine hundred years later, in the fifteenth century? Again, church history proves that the Gospel and Epistle of St. Barnabas were written in the first century and were read in Churches.

The truth seems to be that a Unitarian Gospel of Barnabas did not suit the Trinitarian Christian Creed adopted at the council of Nicaea (325 C.E.) and confirmed at the council of Constantinople (381 C.E.), the Goepel has been given a bad name and hanged in the Decree of Gelasius in the sixth century, and then, not content with even this; its writer dubbed a "renegade" and a "forger", a convenient Peg on which to hang its authorship. That St. Barnabas did write a Gospel is admitted by Christian Chroniclers themselves, e.g., in John Talenets, Nazareums (1718) or Jewish, Gentile and Mohamet on Christianity, containing the

34a. See Introduction of Arabic version of the *Gospel of Barnabas.*
34b. *A History of the Christian* Church by Welliston Walker, pp. 190.

history of the ancient Gospel of Barnabas and the modern Gospel of Mohametans attributed to the same apostle." The only one actually available in the world today is apparently a forgery of the fifteenth century; then where is the one really written by Barnabas, The "Ancient" one and, mind you, condemned not later than the sixth century? "Lost" after the usual pattern, via, "condemnation? Quite obviously, Christendom, whose disregard of history is now too well known to critical scholarship, could not strengthen the truth stated in the Barnabas, and therefore, brought the same disregard of history to bear on this Gospel".[34c]

34c. See, *Christianity in history*, pp.. 30, 32.

(5)

ONE GOD OR THREE?

It is not hard to see that in time this question was bound to arise and to demand an answer. If God is one, how this belief could be held that God is One and at the same time is three. Clement of Rome, who wrote a letter to the Corinthion Church about 97 A.D. says: "As God liveth and the Lord Jesus Christ liveth and the Holy Ghost who are the faith and hope of the elect." (Clem. Rome Ep. ad. Cor. 1, Ch. viii).

At this stage we hear nothing of such terms as "Trinity" or "Person" or "Substance". As yet they were not. even thought of, simply because the need had arisen to call them into existence. But they were proclaiming Christianity to the world as the worshiping of the One true God in opposition to the various idolatrous systems of heathenism with their numerous gods and goddesses. If they called the Father God, and Son God — were they not also open to the charge of believing in more gods than one?

Let us recall again the main point around which discussion centred. There is One God — and yet, Jesus is God. How were two such apparently contradictory statement to be reconciled. And further, how were they to be harmonised with the teaching of the Bible itself, that God is One? If God be one — then it must be the case that Jesus was not really God. He was born in a miraculous way, he ate and drank and was subject to all the physical consequences of eating and drinking. He evinced human infirmities and could not overcome the various demands of nature. This view of the matter was promulgated in Rome about the end of the second century A.D. by a teacher called Artemon; but it is especially associated with the name of Paul of Samosata, who became Bishop of Antioch in 260 A.D. Whatever else may be said of this solution, it clearly gave up the Divinity of Jesus, and so failed to do justice to the teaching of St. Paul-Saul of Tarsus.

"Arius was a Presbyter of Alexandria who lived in the opening years of the fourth century A.D. His teaching rose from a desire to emphasize God's Unity. He sought to do this by asserting that Jesus is a creature — the first indeed of all creatures and the creator of his fellow creatures, but still himself a creature."

"The great opponent of Arius was ATHANASIUS, who afterwards became Bishop of Alexandria. His special service to Christian thought was that, while jealously asserting the Divine Unity, he emphasized the distinctness of the Son from the Father. His great leading thought was that of unity of essence." The Son is and has been for all eternity, of the same essence as the FATHER. It was Athanasius who at the COUNCIL OF NICAE in 325 A.D. had inserted in the creed the word "HOMOOUSIOS" (of one substance with") which was intended to exclude the views both of Sabellius and Arius."

We no doubt, read something to the contrary in St. Mathew, 4:10 "Thou shall worship the Lord thy God, and Him only shalt thou serve." He also says: "The foxes have holes, and the birds of the air have nests, but the Son of Man hath not where to lay his head." Of myself I can do nothing"; 'Of that day and that hour knoweth no man...neither the son" "If any man hear my words and believe not, I judge him not; for I can not to judge the world." I cast out devils by the finger of God" (Luke. 11:20). "I thank thee, O Father, that Thou hast heard me, and I know that Thou hearest me always; but because of the people which stand by I said it that they may believe that Thou hast sent me." (John 11: 42). "The works which the Father hath given me to finish, the same works that I do, bear witness of me, that the Father hath sent me" (John 5:36). "I do nothing of myself". (John 8:28).

In synoptic records, there is enough material in the saying of Jesus himself that enable us to conclude that he was one of the Prophets of God, that he never claimed any kind of Goodhood for himself. When Scribe asked Jesus: "which is the First Commandment of All? And he answered him: The First of all the commandments is, Hear O Israel, the Lord our God is One Lord-And the Scribe said unto him: "Well Master thou hast said the truth, for there is One God, and there is none other but He........and when Jesus saw that he answered discreetly, he said unto him, "Thou art not far from the Kingdom of God" (Mark 12 : 28 : 33).

To me, however, he was a great Prophet, a messenger from God, who lived and tried to uplift his fellowmen. Veiled in a mystery too dense to allow an average eye to penetrate to the realities — that is to say, the everyday bearing of his message, his clarion is still audible. My God and your God is One God. From the pedestal of Divinity, to which ignorance and credulity has raised him, he still says, "Do not call me good, for there is none good but God." The reply of Jesus to the Tempter was that "Thou shalt worship the Lord thy God, and Him only shalt thou serve." (Matt: @ : 10). Contrary to it, St. Paul in all his writings Philo speaks of Logos — a Philosophic Conception of later growth and a development of the "Idea of Plato", in his theory of emanation. Thus St. Paul introduced new logic into Christian Theology, and expressed them in new Phraseology which till today graces all Church Orations. Religious sermons are besprinkled with phrases like the following which Paul and a few others were the first to use in Christian literature "God's First Born"; "The Intercessor with the Father"; "The Image of God"; "The High Priest"; "The Interpreter of God to man"; "The Gift of God"; "Actions without Faith no value".

In the light of St. Paul's New Phraseology, we trace the source of Pauline inspiration. In his Phraseology he is the disciple of Philo and Plato, and not of Jesus. Jesus was a man of action; his days were with man and his nights with God. He was a great believer of Only One Absolute. We find no reconciliation between Jesus as postrayed in the Synoptic — first three Gospels and he Jesus of Pauline writings. Let us look to the Master as the sole guide, and all these differences in the Canonical Gospels and Gospel of Barnabas will come to an easy solution. There is no other course now left to a true Christian after what I have said in these pages.

The doctrine of the Trinity as formulated by the Early Fathers was "added on" to the teaching of the New Testament; it grew by a inevitable process out of Jesus' teaching. Long before the days of Jesus, Plato had perceived that in each individual there is a trinity of reason, spirit and desire. And the Greek theologians who had been trained in the schools of philosophy, constantly use the trinity that there is human nature as the most opposite illustration of that is the Divine Nature.

Our very brief survey of the stages by which the doctorine of the Trinity was gradually formed has brought to light one interesting fact. It was to a large extent the work of men trained in the philosophic Schools of Greece who naturally, in order to express their thoughts, employed words taken over from Greek Philosophy. A clear and brief account of the various Gnostic Schools may be found in Dr. Foakes— Jacksons' History of Christian Church.

If we bear in mind the deep study and devotion with which these early writes regarded the Bible teaching and the scrupulous care with which they followed it, we shall feel the utter improbablity of the notion that they brought the idea of the Trinity into Christianity from other religion. It is true that the gods of India were in some cases worshipped in groups of three; we find similar trinities in the religions of ancient Babylonia, Egyptian and Persian and so forth. Hence, the Christian Trinity was borrowed from one or other of these sources. The Synoptic Gospels received their inspiration more from the Mithraic Cult than from the HOLY GHOST, When they gave us the story of the birth of Jesus.

The author of the Epistle to the Hebrews says, Jesus is only a priest after the order of Melchisedec, "which is king of peace; without father, without mother, without descent, having neither beginning of days nor end of life, but made like unto the Son of God"(Heb. 7:1—3). But Jesus had a mother, had descent, had beginning of days and end of life but Melchisedec had none. Apart from Pauline literature, the Jesus of the Synoptic writing is not Virgin-born. Jesus has been called the son of David. He could not be a descendant of David unless he comes from the loins of Joseph the Carpenter. The genealogy given in the Gospel of St. Mathew and St. Luke says the same thing. The descent of Jesus to Abrahim's is thought the husband of Mary St. Luke is very clear on this point. "And Jesus himself began to be about thirty years of age, being (as we supposed) the son of Joseph which was the son of Heli, "The parenthetical clause is admittedly a subsequent addition. Jesus is believed to have fulfilled in himself some of the prophecies which were made in respect of a descendant of David. If he does not spring from the loins of Joseph, how can those prophecies be fulfilled in him?

Now, I will mention some of the verses that I read in the Bible, and leave it to my readers to decide for themselves whether in the teaching of the Bible is One God or three?

Only One God:

It is set forth as the basis of faith, worship, devotion, obedience and fear:

Hear, O Israel: the Lord our God is One Lord; and thou shalt love the Lord thy God with all thine heart, and with all thy soul, and with all thy might.
(Deut. vi. 4. 5).
This demands a perfect consecration which by the very term only One Object can claim.
Know therefore this day, and consider it in thine heart, that the Lord He is God in heaven above, and upon the earth beneath: there is none else. Thou shalt keep therefore His Statutes. (Deut. iv. 39, 40).
Here supreme obedience is exacted to one sole Authority which can have no rival.
There is no God with Me: I kill, and I make alive: I would, I heal: neither is there any that can deliver out
-of My hand. For I lift up My hand to heaven, and say,
* I live for ever. (Deut. xxxii. 39, 40).
There is only one Judge to be reverenced and feared for time and for eternity.

As a Protest

It is often urged as the protest of the Supreme against false viens of His nature; especially in those passages of Scripture where Divine revelation come into collision with heathenism. Against the Polytheistic Creed and idolatrous practice of the nations the ONE GOD appeals,
Is there a God beside Me? Yes, there is no God
I know not any. (Isa XLiv : 8).

Against Dualism, the belief, not known by name in Scripture, which has taken refuge in the notion of two co-eternal elements of being, passively co-existent or struggling for mastery, the Eternal more than once commands His Prophets to deliver His own testimony. Having its origin in Persia, this notion passed through later Judaism into the heretical sects of Gnosticism, and spent itself out in Manichacism. The God of Israel condescends to utter His protest against this, perhaps the most natural and widespread of all errors.

I am the Lord, and there is none else, I form the light, and create darkness. (Isa. XLv. 6,7).

Here the very terminology of earlier and later Dualism is used, but it is only to declare that no independent origin of evil must be conceived. It may be impossible for the human mind to understand how He is Whom "there is no darkness at all" (1 John, 1:5) could nevertheless create darkness. The only answer is "There is none else" (Isa XLv. 6,7). But darkness and light are also to be understood by what follows, "I make peace, and create evil", The One God is the abolisher of sin by His peace and its Punisher by His evil.

Against Pantheism, which perverts the doctrine of the Divine Unity by making God the seem of all personalities and forces, but not Himself a distinct personality, the Supreme testified.

He that planted the ear, shall He not hear?
He that formed the eye, shall He not see? (Pslam,xciv:9)

This is an apostrophe to the ungodly in the form of an appeal to the One Judge; but it is the Lord's own refutation of Pantheism in all its future or possible forms. Still more expressly, however, is the true Unity of God opposed to this system of false unity in all those passages which speak of the One Creator of all things.

I am the Lord that maketh all things; that stretcheth forth the heavens alone; that spreadeth abroad the/ earth by Myself. (Isa. XVL:24).

Plurality

In spite of this, there is an undertone of mysterious allusion to a plurality of persons within the Godhead. "But this doctrine was unknown to the Hebrew prophets and Christian apostles. The New Catholic Encyclopaedia (1967 edition, vol. Xiv, p. 306) admits that the doctrine of the Holy Trinity is not taught in the Old Testament". It also admits that the doctrine must be dated as from about three hundred and fifty years after the death of Jesus Christ. "So the early Christians who were taught directly by Jesus Christ did not believe that God is a Trinity". (*The truth that leads to Eternal life*. P. 22 Publisher:Watch Tower Bible & Tract Society of New York).

Only One Absolute

The human mind is so constituted as to be unable to conceive of more than one Absolute Being or One Divine Essence in three persons of coequal. The same instinct of man, or constitution of his nature, which prepares him for the disclosure of God is unable to endure more gods than one; the foundation or source of all being cannot, without contradiction, be multiplied. Unity is not an attribute of Deity, not a quality of essence so much as a condition of relation; the Supreme is related to His Interior Self and to His creatures, but, as God, is unrelated. The primary law of thought that predictates the infinite and the Absolute of the Divine Being demands His eternal unity as a necessary postulate.

What is Unity

The term is used only in analogy. Thought there is one Divine Being, the Unity of God is not a unity of kind or person, because there are not individuals of the same. Species; and, therefore, as for other reason, the word is inapplicable to the Divinity. Of all other objects of thought we can imagine fellows or reproductions. But in God there is absolute soleness, SOLEITS: though what lies hidden in the mystery of this essential ONENESS we know but partially.

It is wrong to dogmatise upon the nature of a unity to which we have no parallel, and which we cannot define by comparison or illustration.

The constitution of nature, both physical and moral, confirms this doctrine by innumerable evidence. Unity is stamped upon the entire creation; so clearly that the whole system of science is based upon this presupposition; its latest conclusions pointing to some one primitive and central force, which some in their blind enthusiasm almost deify as the unknown God. And, it is in earthly things, so it is in things spiritual and heavenly. There is one conscience in man, suggesting one law and one LAWGIVER. There is evil, as there is good, but they both pay homage to the Supreme WILL behind them, which is their equal standard. Hence, the erring philosophy of the world, in the better tendencies of the error has seldom been polytheistic or Dualistic; its universal tendency towards Pantheism declares its indestructible conviction of the Unity of God. This has been its share, to carry the principle to the extreme of denying the personality or creaturely existence outside of the ONE and the ALL.

Does all this make him a Prophet and a true teacher and commentator on the old dispensation, or the bringer of a new dispensation? Is he a teacher of a moral or a founder of a Sacrament, the well-established rite of the Pagan world? Dean Inge has very rightly said that the Church named after him was never found by Jesus. If the Pharises and Scribes came, or sent their followers to him, they always did so to test his knowledge in the Mosaic religion, and never looked to him as one who came to found a new faith. I fail to find anything contrary to the above in any of his subsequent utterances throughout his life. Decidedly he brought us new convenant. He laid stress on the Old dispensation, and made entry into the Kingdom of heaven exclusively dependant on the observance of the Old Testament's Laws. He did not preach the religion of "Atonement through Blood", but the religion of "Obedience" and "Commandment". With him the laws was a blessing, and not a curse as St. Paul would make it.

(6)

INCARNATION

The theory of "INCARNATE GOD" is based upon the 6th and 7th verses in the 2nd chapter of St. Paul's Epistle to the Philippious which run as follows:

"Who being in the FORM of God, counted it not a prize to be on equality with God, butemptied himself, taking the form of a servant, being made in the likeness of men."

The sense of these verses, according to Bishop Hall, is as follows:

"Who being very God and knowing it to be no presumption in him to equalize himself to God the Father, yet voluntarily debased and humbled himself."

According to St. Paul, Jesus emptied himself of Godhead and assumed the form of a human being. This self-emptying or "Kenosis" of Jesus in order to assume the form of a servant has given rise to a host of questions:

Logical, Theological, Ethical and Metaphysical; none of which has ever been satisfactorily answered by the worshippers of Jesus. For instance, one notices the utter helplessness of Bishop Charles Gore, D.D., when he says:

"Thus, if we are asked the question, have the functions of the Son in the Godhead and in the universe been suspended by the Incarnation? We cannot but answer with the theologians of the Church from Irenaeus to Dr. West-Cott, that it is to us inconceiveable."

(*Dissertation on subjects connected with Incarnation*, p. 93).

Let us now draw logical inferences from the verses in question:

1. The Logos or the second person, was really God. (John 1:1)
2. This very Logos became 'flesh' (John 1:14).
3. In becoming flesh (man) this Logos "Emptied himself" of his Godhead (Phil. 2:6).

4. This emptied Logos — no more God now assumed the form of a servant and became man. (Phil. 2:7).

Every true, Christian, when kneeling before the Altar, calls Jesus as God — "real God", "equal to the Father in Essense and Nature", "God of God", "Light of Light", and "very God of very God". But St. Paul says this very God, — the Logos — the Son of God, was emptied of Godhead and joined to the physical body of Jesus and remained depotentiated and divested of Godhead throughout his earthly life.

So the question arises:

1. What became of the Godhead?

2. Where did it remain for 33 years?

3. What name should be given to the "very God" after it had emptied itself of Godhead?

4. If the Logos was emptied of Godhead how can the Church affirm that God was crucified?

5. If the Logos was emptied of Godhead, what purpose did it serve by joining itself to the flesh of Jesus?

6. If the Logos — the Son of God — was totally depotentiated, how could Jesus say, "I and my Father are one"?

7. If St. Paul is right, St. John is certainly wrong when he says 'we beheld his glory, the glory as of the only begotten of the Father."(John 1:14).

8. How could John behold the glory of the Son of God when the son of God has been totally emptied of his Godhead before joining the body of Jesus Christ?

9. If St. Paul is right not only the four Gospels, the Nicene Creed, the Thirtynine Articles, the Church and the whole Christian religion became meaningless, but also the Christians throughout the twenty centuries have been labouring under a delusion, i.e. calling a being God who was not God, but devoid of all Godhead.

St. John says that the Logos was God. St. Paul says that the Logos was not God but in the "form of God."

According to St. John, this Logos, who was God, became flesh, i.e. Jesus was God-Incarnate. St. Paul says that this Logos, before being joined to the man Jesus, emptied himself of Godhead, i.e. depotentiated LOGOS "took the form of servant".

Observations

(a) Being God and being in the form of God — these two statements, logically speaking, connote   two different objects. Moreover, it is nowhere recoraed in the New Testament   that the Father was in   the form of God.   The commentators interpret 'form' as meaning 'naturet'. Even so, the Logos, atleast, can be taken as another God besides the Father.

(b) Even   conceding   Godhead to the Logos, one cannot reconcile St. John with St. Paul as the latter affirms that the Logos — the Son — divested himself completely of His divinity before assuming the form of a servant.

"Though existing before the worlds in the eternal Godhead, yet he did not cling with avidity   to the prerogatives of his Divine majesty, did not display his equality with God, but divested himself of the glories of heaven and took upon himself the nature of a servant and appeared among men in the fashion of a man." (Bishop Lightfoots: *Commentary to the Phillippions.* p. 108).

Leaving the Christians to reconcile these two contradictory   statements at leisure, I now proceed to enumerate some of the questions that logically arise in this connection:

1. Did the   Logos   empty himself of his divinity out of his own free will or did somebody else, e.g. the Father effect this depotentiation?

2. If the   Logos   (son) and the Fahter both are one and the same Being, in other words, if there is only one God without a second, was the Father also depotentiated automatically?

3. If the answer to this question is in the affirmative, where did the Godhead go? If in the negative, are there not proved two distinct gods thereby, one retaining His Divine form intact, and the other standing divested of His Godhead entirely?

4. If the Logos is also God, is it logically possible for a God to become non-God and yet to retain his Godhead in such a way as not to disturb the economic trinity?

5. Self-emptying or Kenosis is a change not only in the form but in the essence; and God is supposed by the Christians to be immutable.

"This immutability of God is intimately connected with His immensity and eternity; and is frequently included with them in the scriptural statements concerning His nature.... As an infinite and absolute Being, Self-existent and absolutely independent, God is exalted above all the causes and even above the possibilities of change. Infinite space and infinite duration cannot change. So God is absolutely immutable in His essence and attributes. He can neither increase nor decrease. He is subject to no process of development ." (Systematic Theology, vol. 1, p. 390, by Dr. Charles Hodge).

Now, if all this is true, certainly the second person in the Trinity, by emptying himself of his Divinity, did undergo a radical change, hence he is no more God; if so, the doctrine of the Trinity falls to the ground.

(6) The Logos — the Son of God and the second person in the Trinity, when he emptied himself of his Godhead and assumed the nature of a man thereby acquired human consciousness, as is evidenced by the Gospel records. He was neither omniscient nor omnipotent. This means that for 33 long years — the earthly life of Logos — there were only two persons in the Trinity, the Father and the Holy Ghost. Thus the Doctrine of the Trinity is thrown to the winds.

(7) The Logos was the Son of God. This Logos emptied himself of his Godhead. Well and good. Now I ask, what

name shall we give to this emptied being, God or non-God? If God, St. Paul stands condemned, as he says that the Logos emptied himself of his Divinity altogether. If non-God, then St. John is certainly in the wrong, as he says, that God became flesh.

(8) If the Logos before assuming the form of a servant (before becoming man), divested himself of his Divinity completely, as St. Paul would have us believe, St. Athanasius is certainly in the wrong when he says that Jesus Christ is perfect God plus perfect man. Jesus Christ, according to St. Paul, is just the reverse of perfect God, he is no more God.

(9) If the Logos is God and this Logos was joined to the man Jesus, Divinity and humanity must exist side by side.
    (a) If both Divinity and humanity underwent a fusion (as the Church believes), then Jesus is neither man nor God but something else.
    (b) If both these attributes existed side by side, Jesus must be omniscient, but the Gospels state that he was not.

(10) The Logos is God, Jesus is man. Very well, but the fusion of the two into one whole is metaphysically impossible as God is a necessary Being and man a contingent being, and the amalgamation of the two is a metaphysical impossibility.

(11) St. John nowhere says that the Logos emptied himself of his Divinity, but St. Paul does so. The question is: both cannot be right at one and the same time; hence the New Testament is not the revealed word of God.

(12) The Logos, according to St. Paul divested himself of his Divinity. Did he ever afterwards regain his divine majesty? If he did, how? He was depotentiated and as such had no power left in him. If he did not, where was his divinity reposing? If the Father came to his help; when? And if so, are there not proved two Gods thereby, one in His majesty and the other in stark nakedness?

(13) The New Testament says that Logos is the sustainer of the universe: as he is the son of God. But after the Kenosis, how could he exercise his Divine majesty as there was none left with him, and how could he control this universe? If he could, then he did not empty himself and if the Fathter performed the function in his stead, his being is proved superfluous. We can very well do with two gods only — the Father and the Holy Ghost.

(14) All the Church Fathers (Canonized by the Church) affirm that Jesus is absolutely God. Dr. Liddon says that "We believe that Jesus is absolutely God." (Our Lord's Divinity p. 226). But St. Paul says that the Logos joined himself to the man Jesus not as absolute God but as depotentiated God, which virtually amounts to no God at all. Certainly the Church has throughout these twenty centuries, been groping in the dark.

(15) What is the relation between the depotentiated Logos and the man Jesus?

(a) Was this Logos a substitute for the human soul Jesus? If so, Jesus cannot be styled "perfect man", for man is a mixture of body and soul, as such the Athanasian Creed falls to the ground. If not, then there were two active principles in one man, Viz: a human soul and a Divine Logos. How did they adjust themselves in one person and what purpose, cosmic, ethical or divine, did this depotentiated Logos serve? And what about the consciousness of Jesus? Was it human or Divine

If it was human, was the Divine in him sleeping? and if Divine, why did Jesus say 'I do not know when the Hour would come?" There are many utterances of Jesus denoting his human consciousness. Consequently the Logos element served no purpose at all.

Jesus says, "My father is greater than I." If this statement is true, why did his Divinity not assert itself? If it was subordinated to his humanity, it is no divinity at all.

(b) The Logos before entering the corporal body of Jesus divested himself of his Godhead, if St. Paul is to be believed at all. If so, Jesus cannot be styled perfect God.

(c) If the Father and the Son both are one and the same being, did the former also join Himself to the body of the Jesus?

(d) If humanity and Divinity both existed simultaneously in one person, that person is neither God nor man but a different one altogether.

(16) If the Logos became joined to Jesus in the place of the human soul, Jesus is not a real human being and if he possessed a soul as well, this soul could not assert itself in the presence of the Logos.

(b) If the Logos existed side by side with the soul, the question is what relation did it have with Jesus? Moreover, in one man we have two personalities, human and Divine; and as a fusion of these elements is impossible, Jesus had a dual personality and the Gospel's records become an enigma.

(c) The Logos before being joined to Jesus had emptied himself of his Divinity, so it is quite wrong to say that Jesus Christ was God.

(17) When and how did this depotentiated Logos regain his Divine majesty?" If before the crucifixtion, please quote the chapter and verse of the Gospels; and explain how could God die? God, as we know, cannot die. If after the crucifixion, then only a man was crucified and he being a sinner by nature could not atone for the sins of mankind.

(18) Is it logically possible for God to denude Himself of His Divinity? and can we conceive of a God who can empty Himself of Godhead. To call such a being — God is certainly a misnomer — rather contradiction in terms.

(19) According to the Nicene Creed, Jesus is the very God and there is only one God; so can we say that this Kenosis is applicable to the Father as well?

(20) How did depotentiated Logos regain his consciousness? himself or through the agency of the Father? Please quote the New Testament in support of your suppositions.

(21) If the Kenotic theory is right, then the Athanasian Creed absolutely wrong. For the latter teaches that two

perfect natures i.e. the Godhead and manhood, were joined together in one person. Whereas, St. Paul says that the Logos emptied Himself of His Godhead before being joined to the man Jesus. Hence two perfect natures were not present in Jesus Christ.

(*The Three Creeds* by Gibron, p. 221).

These questions which can be still further multiplied have baffled the most acute intellects of Christendom from Iraneus down to our times and the luminaries and dignitaries of the Church have expressed such contradictory views regarding this theory and its logical implications that their perusal is sure to baffle and bewilder even the ordinary student of Church history or the history of Christian doctrines. Below I quote a few of the well-known Church fathers and teachers in support of my statement.

(a) The Logos is the mediator between God and the World; says Origen, and "He is personal." Further "He is generated of the Father who is God in himself and the Logos (Son) is the second God, a kind of repetition or "duplicate of God". He is of another substance.

Further, 'Jesus is possessed of a human soul in inseparable unity with the Logos". "The human nature of Jesus is not unaffected by its indissoluble union with the divine Logos."

(*History of Christian Doctrine* by Dr. G.P. Fisher).

If Origen is right, the whole superstructure built upon the Nicene Creed — the whole Christian Church — tumbles down like a house of cards.

(i) Father is the God — the Logos is God.

(ii) The essence of the Father is different from that of Logos.

Moreover, the Human soul of Jesus is inseparable united with the Logos, the mixture is neither human nor Divine. Hence Jesus is neither God nor man.

(b) Cerinthus rejected Origen and says that the Logos left Jesus at the time of his baptism.

(c) Sabellius says that Logos, Father and Holy Ghost are one and the same being. If the Logos is distinct personality then there would be two Gods, which is logically impossible.

(d) Arius held that the Logos (The Son) is inferior in rank to God the Father, and his essence is different from that of the Father

Observations

Arius says exactly the same thing as Origen, but it is surprising to note that poor Arius was excommunicated and declared a heretic while his teacher (Origen) was not condemned by the Church, although we know, he is the author of the theory of subordination.

(e) Tertullian says that the Logos is not eternal: "there was a time when he was not", i.e. the Logos is a created being.

(f) Mani held that the body of Jesus was a mere phantom, he had no human soul at all, as it is logically impossible to unite God with man.

(g) Apollinarius taught that Jesus had a real body and the Logos was substitute for human soul, as two natures human and Divine could not exist side by side in one person.

(h) Nestorious believed that Jesus was mere man but had the spark of divinity in his nature. He does not believe in the Logos theory at all.

(i) Entyches was of opinion that Jesus had but one Divine nature, as be was one person, and two natures can not subsist in one person.

(j) Clement says that the Logos "was very near to God, he was not God, he was not God in the real sense."

(k) Theophilus and Terullian, in concaternate sub-ordinationism of their doctrine of the Logos and with a view to preserving both the philosophical idea of God as supramundance and the reality of the Biblical theophanies, resolved the idea of Gods' becoming visible into the idea that the Logos was a "second God" who was not equal to "the uncaused Father". Thus these Church Fathers affirm their belief in pure ditheism.

(l) God the Father is God by His very nature; He is uncaused; God the Son is God through generation; he is also God but owes his being to the Father.

(m) Iraneus says that the Logos is becoming man, imposed self-limitation upon his Divinity as without this God could not assume the form of man.

(n) Iraneus asserts that the Incarnation did not interrupt the cosmic activity of the Word.

"He was made man," he says, "While all the same existing in the world and invisibly sustaining all creation." (*Dissertations*, by Bishop Gore, p. 99). In other words this pious father would have us believe that though the Logos emptied himself of his Godhead yet he did not cease to be God! Credulity, logical absurdily, can go no further.

(o) Eusebius says that, "The Word became incarnate in order to press spiritual and rational realities to us; but in doing this his own divine nature was subjected to no change." (Bishop Gore, *Dissertations*, p. 101).

This is against the plain teaching of St. Paul, who affirms that the word in becoming man subject his equality with God.

(p) Athanasius asserts, "Incarnation did not limit the word (Logos) in himself. He is an still in the universe and in the bosom of the Father." (Bishop Gore, *Dissertations*, p. 103).

He too teaches something contrary to St. Paul who affirms the word (Logos) did not impose self-limitation upon himself in becoming man.

(q) Proclus says, "He, the same, was in his father's bosom and in the womb of the Virgin. He was being worshipped by the angels in heaven and was supping with publicans on earth. Here (on earth) he was being maligned as a cheat while there (in heaven) he was being glorified as God." (*Dissertations* by Bishop Gore p.104).

Here we have a strange picture of Jesus. He was a human being on earth and a God in heaven at one and the same time. "There is nothing in the New Testament," rightly contends Gore, "to justify this sort of language."

(r) Now listen to Origen.

First, there is only one God. Secondly, that Jesus Christ, born of the Father before all creatures, emptied himself of His glory, became man and was incarnate, although God while made man, remained the God which he was."

This "greatest Church teacher of the East" indulges in logical absurdities which certainly ill become a theologian of his calibre. He says that the Son of God emptied himself of his Divine glory yet remained the God which he originally was! If this is admissible, we can as well say that this tumbler is empty yet full of water! If Jesus really remained God, how could he grow in wisdom as taught by St. Luke?

Bishop Gore is also confused at these divergent views and says "that there were different opinions and tones of thought of this great subject in the second century."

(*Dissertations* by Bishop Gore, p. 121).

Is it right to worship God in visible forms in the form of images and idols? It is contended sometimes that a visible image helps to concentrate attention. Upon a visible image you can fix the gaze of your external physical eye only. As soon as you try to turn the light of your inward, mental eye upon any subject, the external eye ceases to gaze upon external objects. It refuses to focus itself on them, and if you insist on fixing your gaze, the inward eye will refuse to function and your mind will refuse to think and meditate. Far from being a help, therefore, an external object, an image or an idol is a means of hindrance to concentration of the mind and purity of worship. God is UNSEEN. He is not something upon which the phsycial eye could be made to rest. God is spirit and can be worshipped only in spirit, with the mind and soul only.

Jesus, indeed, came to demolish the paganism and not to reproduce it under his name, as the Church after his name did. He said to Pagan woman that he was "not sent but unto the lost sheep of the house of Israel." (Matt. 15.24); and being pressed, only added: It is not meant to take the children's bread and to cast it to dogs"(Matt. 15:26).

Dean Inge has very rightly said that the Church named after him was never founded by Jesus. If the Pharisees and Scribes came, or sent their followers to him, they always did so to test his knowledge in the Mosie religion, and never looked to him as one who came to found a new faith. Decidedly he brought no new covenant. He laid stress on the Old dispensation, and made entry into the kingdom of heaven exclusively dependent on the observance of the Law. He did not preach the religion of "Atonement through Blood" but the religion of Repentance and Obedience. He gave his religion in the following words·

"Think not that I am come to destroy the law, or the Prophets: I am not come to destroy, but to fulfil. For verily I say unto you, till heaven and earth pass, one jot or one tittle shall in no wise pass from the law, till all be fulfilled. Whosoever therefore shall break one of these least commandments and shall teach men so, he shall be called the least in the kingdom of heaven; but whosoever shall do and teach them, the same shall be called great in the kingdom of heaven."

(Matthew 5: 17—19).

(7)

IS JESUS THE SON OF GOD?

The Christian Apologists claim that the Gospel of Barnabas is totally different from the four canonical gospels, and base their claim on the facts that

(1) Barnabas recognises Jesus as a mere prophet and does not recognise him as divine

(2) He does not recognise the doctrine of Atonement, but on the contrary the recognises God as Only One and recognises Jesus as a prophet. But when we compare the synoptic Gospels with the Gospel of Barnabas, we see no difference between them and find that the source of both seems to be one and the same. We may discuss the following points to prove our claim.

(1) Do the synoptic Gospels prove the Divinity of Jesus?
(2) Did Jesus come·to Atone for the sins of all mankind?
(3) Did Jesus believe in the Trinity or in the Oneness of God?
(4) Did Jesus ascribe any of the Messianic Prophecies to himself or did he ever claim to be the Messiah?

In fact, the Jews were anxious to hear Jesus claim to be the Messiah up to the very last moment of his life, but he had always disappointed them, which led them to crucify him, for they thought that he was a false prophet. Now, he can Barnabas be found as guilty if he does not recognise him as the Messiah? Yes, he would have recognised him as such if he had been a Muslim.

The doctrines of Trinity and Atonement do not belong to the Bible, they belong to churchnity. From very early days of the Church there existed such groups that accepted Jesus as only a prophet, and such groups still exist. Neither do they recognise him as Divine nor do they believe in the Atonement. It is only followers of Paul who recognise the law as a curse and regard Jesus as accursed, though they recognise him, at the same time as God and believe in the Atonement.

We want to make it clear to our readers that the prophecies of Barnabas about the Holy Prophet (p.b.u.h.) are not a matter to be wondered at, for God has promised Abraham saying — "And as for Ishmael, I have heard thee. Behold, I have blessed him, and made him fruitful, and will multiply him exceedingly. Twelve princes shall be beget, and I will make him a great nation."

Under the light of this Divine Promise, the prophethhood of Muhammad (p.b.u.h.) is a matter of certainty. We shall, however, discuss this matter in separate book.

Now, in connection with the questions given above, we remark as follows:

Now, since Barnabas had never heard from Jesus that he was God or Son of God or that in Godhood there are three persons and that he was one of the persons, how could he be blamed for avoiding to mention these claims. In fact, he only says that Matthew, Mark, Luke and John have said.

Barnabas analized that Jesus only thought like a man, ate and slept like a man and was subject to all human needs and emotions, such as grief, happiness, laughter and shedding of tears. There are, however, certain remarks made by John that may be ascribed to divinity, but they are mere metaphors not unfamiliar to the Eastern mind. Thus St. Barnabas analized that Jesus was a mortel to all intents and purposes, and shared his origin in common with the other Prophets No student of the Bible can honestly deny the truth of this remark. Jesus ate and drank and was subject to all the physical consequences of eating and drinking. He evinced human infirmities and could not overcome the various demands of nature. He was subject to all human needs and emotions, such as grief, happiness and weeping. St. John tells us that God is a Spirit,[35] whom we cannot see and touch.

The words "Son of God", in Judaic terminology meant nearness to God only. The God of the house of Jacob used the same language: "Israel is my son, even my first born", said God through Moses,[36] so He called David and

35. *John.* 4:24.
36. *Exod.* 4:22.

Solomon.[37] The Judges were called even "God" by David,[38] and fatherless children were given the consolation to take God as their father.[39] If the Judges were the children of the Most High, the wicked were also the same through rebellion.[40] With literature pregnant with such phraseology, under which God has been addressed as Heavenly Father by all Christians, one fails to understand how anyone can claim a special kind of Divinity as has been done for the son of Mary, simply because he was also called "Son of God". These are expressions that would rather establish the Brotherhood of man under the Fatherhood of God than any claim of divinity for Jesus.

St. Luke argues that Jesus was the son of God because of his having been conceived and born without the agency of a father.[41] I will not refer here to what we read in the Mystery cult. If Jupiter in the Pagon world could be the father of "Parcel of sons" through virgin birth, God could be born at least once through a virgin birth. In such words Justin Martyr meets the taunt of the Pagans as to the birth of God in Jesus.

At the appearance of Jesus there were temples without end dedicated to Gods like Apollo or Dionysus among the Greeks, Hercules among the Romans, Mithra among the Persians, Adonis and Attis in Syria and Phrygia; Osiris, Isis and Horus in Egypt; Baal and Astorte among the Babylonians and Carthaginians, and so forth.

All these Deities were sun-gods, and of all or nearly all of them, as Edward Carpenter says, it was believed that:[42]
(1) They were born on or very near Christmas Day.
(2) They were born of a Virgin Mother.
(3) And in a cage or underground chamber.
(4) They led a life of toil for mankind.
(5) They were called by the names of Light-Bringer, Healer, Mediator, Saviour and Deliverer.
(6) They were, however, vanquished by the Power of Darkness.

---

37. Pslams, 89:27.
38. Psalms, 82:6.
39. Psalams, 68:5.
40. Isa, 30:1.
41. Luke, 1:35.
42. *The Sources of Christianity,* p. 89—90.

(7) They descended into Hell or the under world

(8) They rose again from the dead, and became the Pioneers of mankind to the Heavenly World.

(9) They founded communions of Saints and Chruches, to which disciples were received by baptism.

(10) They were commemorated by Eucharistic meals."

The story of the Lord of Christianity is not the first of its kind. Mithraism came from Persia and reached Rome about 70 B.C. Mithra was believed to be a great Mediator between God and man. His birth took place in a cave on December 25th. He was born of a virgin. He travelled far and wide; he had twelve disciples; he died in the service of humanity. He was buried, but rose again from the tomb. His resurrection was celebrated with rejoicing.[43] He was called Saviour, and sometimes figured as a *Lamb*. People were initiated into his cult through baptism. Sacramental feasts were held in his remembrance. St. Jerome and other Early Fathers became puzzled at the similarity existing between Christianity and Mithraism, but their ingenuity ascribed it to the machinations of the Devil to mock their faith.[44]

St.Jerome admits that Mithra and Baal were the same,and called the sons of the Lord. He says: "The Sun whom the heathen worship under the names of Lord Sun (Baal Samus) and the Son of the Lord Borberas.[45] Dean Farrar, in his *Life of Christ*, has very rightly remarked that there are no satisfactory proofs to locate the birth of Jesus on December 25th. The Gospels are silent on the subject, though it makes mention of the Shapherds being that night with their flocks in the fields of Bethlehem.[46] It makes it more difficult to accept December 25th as the real date of the Nativity, December being the height of the rainy season in Judaea, when neither flocks nor shepherds could have been by night in the fields of Bethiehem.

Vesenēr says that the Feast of Nativity was held originally on January 6th (the Epiphany), but in A.D.353-4

43. *Pagan Christ* by Robertson, p. 338.
44. *Our Sun Gods*, p. 179, From Tertullian
45. *Justin Martyr*, Apol. 11.
46. *Hastings. Ency. of Rel. and Ethics*, art. "Christmas".

the Pope Libesius altered it to December 25th, but there is
no evidence of a Feast of the Nativity taking place at all
before the fourth century A.D. It was not until A.D. 534
that Christmas Day and Epiphany were reckoned by the Law-
Courts as "Dies Non."

The Greek Church, even today, does not observe Christmas on December 25th but on January 7th. It was, however, not until the year A.D. 530 or thereabouts that a Scy-
thian monk, Dionysius Exiginus, on about and astronomer,
of Rome, was commissioned to fix the date and the year of
the birth of Jesus. He, it was, who assigned the day, and the
date and the month now accepted in Christendom. The said
monk does not give the date that authorized him to fix
December 25th as the day of the Nativity, but the very date,
within a day or two, is the date of the supposed birth of
many of the Sun-gods. The birth of almost all the Sun-Gods
Apollo, Bacchus, Hercules, Mithra, Adonis, Attis, Osiris,
Horus, Baal, Quetzalcoatl from virgin Mothers, and on the
same date, or within a day or two thereof; the massacre of
the innocents at that time and the flight into a distant
country; the death through crucifixion or otherwise; but
always by the enemies of light and for the benefit of
humanity; the coming of the weeping virgins to the grave; the
empty grave; the resurrection; almost all of the gods
accepted as redeemers of mankind and mediators between
God and man. Had Jesus been one of the Sun-Gods, as he
has been portrayed by his followers — the position isquite
tenable. But this great Messenger of Allah came to demolish
Paganism, as the Qur'an says. His church says the same. His
story should be quite different and distinct from that of the
deities of the ancient days. Let St. Augustine speak: "We
hold this (Christmas) day holy, not like the Pagans, because
of the birth of the Sun, but because of the birth of Him who
made it."

The German Scholar, Dr. Arnold Meyer, Professor of
Theology, University of Zurich has written a book on the
subject. It has also been translated into English and is called
Jesus or Paul. Therein the learned Professor proves con-
clusively that the Godhead of Jesus and the Atonement

are doctrines which owe their origin to the ingenuity of Paul and of which both Jesus and his disciples were totally ignorant."(182).

Jesus did not declare that he had come as a founder of a new religion nor did he formulate any Articles of Faith. He deals only with the spiritual side of life and offers no solution to the material side. For instance, he offers no solution to industrial relation, family life, nor does he advocate any economic doctrine. Christianity has no social philosophy although there are some Christians who call themselves Christian Socialists.

Thus, earliest Christians saw no necessity for organisation, for they regarded this world as a temporary thing which speedily ends with the second coming of their Master. But Jesus did not appear, and the Christians gradually had to adjust themselves to the practical side of the life that since hundreds of years might elapse before the second coming of Jesus, it was essential to develop a definite Church organisation. This led to the setting up of the Present Modern Church.

The worship in the early church was on the pattern of the Jewish church. Gradually, however, the Church service was transformed into beautiful and significant copy of a Roman Temple. Following the growth of church organisation and the crystallization of its dogmas, Church now constitutes the indispensable intermediary between God and man and the Pope claims that his pronouncements are infallible. Its rituals consists of singing accompanied by the choir and the burning of incense especially among the High Church in order to create a sort of rapture in the mind. The simple service of worship became a liturgical rite suffused with spiritual symbolism and central in the life of the Church. The Mass and Baptism became important sacraments of purification. Other elements added to the rituals were the generation of the Saints, Penance and Confession. Baptism in the primitive Church, as we can see from Paul's letters, was into the name of Jesus only, and the verses which contain the command to make disciples of all nations and baptise in the Name of Father and of the Son, and of the Holy Ghost, were additions thus pointed to comparatively late date for the Gospel. These contain reference to the practices of the Church rather than a literal report of the word of Jesus.

The Early Church and the New Testament (pp. 160—262) namely Matthew, Mark, Luke and John selected by a majority vote (*Age of Reason* by Thomas Pain, p. 192), under the Chairman, the Bishop of Rome who had the Emperor Constantine at his back to support him. Those who represent the true religion of One God, were a small minority and though they vehemently opposed all abominations, they were, on pain of torture and death, forced into silence.

The author of the Epistle to the Hebrews says that Jesus is only a priest after the order of Melchizedek, who was "made like unto the son of God."[47] Jesus had a mother, had descent, had, beginning of days and end of life, but Melchizedek had none. Apart from Pauline literature, the Jesus of the Synoptic writings is not virgin born. "The angel of the Lord appeared unto him in a dream, saying, Joseph, thou son of David, fear not to take thee Mary thy wife. for that which is conceived in her is of the Hoy Ghost".[48] For this reason St. Barnabas refused to believe that Jesus was the Messiah. If he could not be a descendant of David, how could he come from the ioins of Joseph, the Carpenter? The descent of Jesus from Abraham is through the husband of Mary. Jesus is believed to have fulfilled in himself some of the prophecies which were made in respect of a descendant of David. If he does not spring from the loins of Joseph, how can those prophecies be fulfilled in him?

The birth of Jesus, if accepted to have occurred as the popular Christian belief has it, is again, not peculiar to him. Because, the Divinity of Christ does not of necessity imply virgin birth. If it could be historically proved, it would be no demonstration of Christ's Divinity, nor would disproof of it through any doubt on the doctrine. In the Bible we read of other births without parents. Adam was from God, and has been styled "Son of God" by Luke; Jesus had a mother, but Adam was without any parent. And the same may be said of Melchizedek. Whether the forerunner is for us entered, even Jesus, made an high priest for ever after the order of Melchizedek.

47. Heb. 7:1—3.
48. Mat. 1:20.

Jesus came like the other "begotten sons of God", to reclaim a fallen race which had once been redeemed through Moses. Like other Prophets, he came to reclaim humanity at a time when it had turned aside from God. Jesus met the same opposition that awaits every reformer in his own days. He met the same persecution which comes to the fate of every martyr of truth. His tribe had gone astray from the path of righteousness, and unpalatable to the unrighteous. The Rabbis were exposed, and the hollowness of the Pharisees shown. He thus incurred hatred of his own people, who began to plot his death, and this brought him to the cross. The fate of Jesus is the fate of every martyr of the right cause. He taught what he thought could reconcile a sinful man to the Creator. People had become accustomed "to clean the outside of the cup or platter", but he exhorted them to think more of cleaning their hearts. This was something new to everybody, and a new testament for the remission of sins. But the establishment of this seemingly new teaching demanded a very great sacrifice. He could not establish these principles of righteousness and godliness without obeying the Father. Because, the reformation has never been worked out without the persecution of its advocates.

This should be borne in mind that Jesus came to demolish Paganism and not to reproduce it under his name as being the LIFE GIVER through blood. If Jesus came to make us "free from sin", and we became the servants of righteousness, why should he enjoin every person to teach the law and observe the Commandments? To the young man who came to him and asked how could he gave eternal life, Jesus speaks of the Ten Commandments and orders him to observe them. In the same way he refers his own disciples to the Scribes, for they "are in the seat of Moses". In all his utterances there is not a single word which may give countenance to the theory of atonement. Much had been made of some of his words at his last Passover — "For this is my blood of the New Testament which shed for many for the remission of sins." The words are simple, and do not carry any meanings to an Eastern mind, which favour the new dispensation of the "blood". Jesus came like the other "Prophets" to reclaim a fallen race which had once been redeemed through Moses.

According to the Holy Qur'an, we Muslims accept Jesus as a messenger from God, and regard him as one entitled to our allegiance, even as our own Prophet. We cannot do otherwise in the face of the Holy Qur'an:

"Says: We believe, in Allah and (in) that which has been revealed to us; and (in) that which was revealed to Abraham and Ismail and Issac and Jacob and the tribes, and (in) that which was given to Moses and Jesus, and (in) that which was given to the Prophets from their Lord; we do not make any distinction between any of them, and to Him do we submit." (2:136).

Thus, we make no distinction between Muhammad (S.A.W.) and the other Prophets. Nay, I can safely say, that our love for Jesus is in no case less than that cherished for him by those who pass under his name; and in a sense, our regard for and devotion to him are more than that shown by his own followers. If Jesus, for the sake of árgument, was neither God nor His Son in the sense in which the church in the West accepts him, would It not be a sort of infatuation, bringing him under a unintentional libel. It is a disgrace, and not an honour, to call any person a son of a king, when he is not.

No doubt some of his expressions have caused difficulty to many in appreciating the true mission of Jesus. In interpreting them, we should not forget that Jesus was from the East. We Easterners think in metaphors and speak in similes when we wish to become emphatic. An intelligent study of the other Prophets from the East will show that Jesus did not speak of some exclusive possession, he spoke as other Prophets had spoken in different accents and stresses. Any person who believed that man was created after the image of God would use, as Jesus did, the expression "the Father sent me". Every man possesses divine elements in him, so the Qur'an says. All that is noble and good in us is of God, and so God is in us. In the same way the Father was in Jesus. "No men cometh to the Father but by me", is another expression which Jesus had used, and so have the others. Prophets always make their appearance at a time when humanity is at its lowest ebb, morally and spiritually. They come to reclaim it. They find man estranged from God, and they come to bring him back to his Lord. People are groping in the dark wilderness of wickedness, and Prophets hold the torch of light to righteousness and virtue. They walk humbly with God, and one who cares to approach his Creator must follow them. Is not, then, the Prophet of the moment justified in saying, just as Jesus said:"No man cometh to the Father but by me". Every Prophet in his own time can say so if he, and only he, has been raised in his time by God to bring others to him. The same has been spoken of the Prophet Muhammad in the Qur'an :

"Say, If you love God, then follow me. God will love you and forgive you your faults." (3:30).

Paul did not go to the Gentiles with the word of Jesus, who did not preach the doctrine of Atonement through Blood, "But the religion of Obedience and Comamndment". With him the law was a blessing and not a curse as Paul would make it. Paul went to the Gentiles to repeat their own story in their own language. He established a new Politico-economic system in the name of Jesus. The Prophets of democracy sought to establish the dignity of men and presented the slogan of Liberty, Equality and Fraternity. The Communist Pundits talk of equal distribution of wealth, equal opportunities and equal sharing of profits. Paul prescribed equal distribution of Jesus through Faith, Hope and Charity. In fact, Paul had no intention of preaching the teachings of Jesus. All that he wanted was to establish a kingdom of his own that he could rule over, for he loved power and glory for himself.

Discussing the state of affairs in the contemporary Middle East, Bertrand Russell says: "It depends for its stability upon religion and the divinity of the King. Disobedience was impiety, and rebellion was liable to call down anger of gods. Paul had recognised this fact. His physical inadequacy prevented him from becoming a warrior and achieving glory through conquests like Alexander or other Roman Emperors, so he chose his own ground to fight with the object of achieving power and glory. Hence, Paul chose the ground of his operations in religion — his target, the Gentiles, his weapon, incarnation of Jesus Christ, his arsenal, Mithraism, Platonism and of course Judaism, and his method "While in Rome do as the Romans do." Indeed expediency was the greatest principle of his tactics." And unto the Jews I became as a Jew that I might gain the Jews; to them that are as under the law, that I might gain them that are without law as without law", (being not without law to God, but under the law to Christ.)

"For if the truth of God hath more abounded through my lie unto his glory, why yet am I also judged as a sinner? And not rather (as we be slanderously reported, and as some affirm that we say), let us do evil, that good may come? Whose damnation is just.

In short Paul preached a gospel that was not taught by Jesus. Had Paul not taken the liberty with law and propagated his own doctrine and philosophy, Jesus would have been included among the true prophets of Israel. But he sacrificed the real Jesus at the altar of his ambition. He created a mythical Jesus to adorn his personality and lend power to his speech. He pretended to speak from the tongue of his Lord Jesus. He defied and ignored, kept himself aloof from St. Barnabas and also from the other apostles.

In fact, Jesus himself never claimed Godhood. On the other hand, he said "Thou shall worship the Lord thy God, and Him only shall thou serve". In the language of metaphor Jesus said: "And no man hath ascended up to heaven, save the son of man, who is in heaven." Jesus, as a Jew, did believe that at least two men, Enoch and Elijah, had ascended into heaven, and therefore, he could not say that no man has ascended into heaven, and therefore, he could not say that no man has asended into heaven. Jesus at the time of this utterance was not in heaven, he was on the earth.

To sum up I say that St. Barnabas was without doubt admittedly one of the ordained disciples of Jesus, who saw Jesus, touched him, remained in his company, sat with him, heard his Sermons, wrote down his sermons under his directions. Further, he did produce a Gospel based on words, sayings and teachings of Jesus. That this Gospel was in vogue upto the time it was officially proscribed and banned by the order of Constantine and the Pope later on. Why this Gospel and the epistles of St. Barnabas were proscribed and banned has not been explained anywhere so far. Those were written in Aramaic, the spoken and written language of Jesus.

The story of the present Gospel of Barnabas alleged to
be the work of other than Barnabas, has not so far been
authentically repudiated by bringing forward the real and
original Gospel of Barnabas or any other counter Gospel of
Barnabas in Aramaic language, and unless such a book is
produced, exmained and scrutinized minutely, there cannot
be any convincing reason to challenge the validity and
authenticity of the present Gospel of Barnabas though
thousands of objections and explanations may be put
forward. The present Gospel of Barnabas alleged to be in
Italian and found by Fra-Marino is said to be a translation
of the original Gospel of St. Barnabas — where is this original
to? The Christians who thoroughly know the evolutionary
history of the four current Gospels of Matthew, Mark, Luke
and John, do know that all of them were completed long
after the death of Jesus; that no conclusive proof has been
put forward that those are the very gospels which are
produced on the base of words, sayings and teachings of
Jesus. The authors of those gospels do not claim even to have
seen Jesus. It is irony of fate that these gospels are being presented as the canonical gospels while the Real Gospel —
Gospel of Barnabas — has been banned, declared as forged
and removed from the face of the earth.

(8)

CHRISTIAN INVENTION

Forgery:

"For there are three that bear record in heaven, the
Father, the WORD, and the Holy Ghost; and these three
are one."[47]

This verse, being demonstrated a Forgery, is omitted
from the Revised version. It is the only text distinctly
asserting the doctrine of the Trinity, which is really a
Christian invention or development of later date than the
Bible.

Says H. S. Reimasus that "Our Christianity rests upon
a Fraud,"[48] quoted by Albert Schweitzer in "Quest of
Historical Jesus", p. 22.

47. John, 5:7.
48. *Quest of Historical Jesus of Albert Schweltzer.* p. 22.

On the contrary, Christian Apologists say that the Gospel according to Barnabas is forged by a Muslim convert. And a most audacious feat on the part of Christianity!

"How audacious the thief, for he holds a lamp in his hand".

In order to know the fact — And all I can do here is to borrow, as I quote the Christianity in History "The case of this Gospel of St. Barnabas is interesting and instructive, and must be described at some length, to give the reader an idea of how Christianity has treated its records — "treated" in both senses of the word, First of all, let us have a look at the most famed, and acknowledgedly the best informed general book in Christiandom, The Encyclopaedia Britannica, under the heading "Apocryphal literature"'is an entry:

Gospel of Barnabas—condemned in the Gelasian Decree (Decretum Gelasianum).

Decretum Gelasianum is described as "a compilation of documents anterior to St. Gregory (C. 540—C.604) and it is difficult to determine Gelasius contributions to it; at all events, as we know it, it is of Roman origin and sixth century or later". Gelasius is explained as "Gelasius, St. confirmed the estrangement between the Eastern and Western churches by insisting on the removal of the name of Acacius, bishop of Constantinople, from the diptychs."[49]

In the first place, if the Gelasian Decree is anterior to St. Gregory, who died in C. 604, then it cannot be "later" than the sixth century except by a maximum of four or five years. In any case it would be anterior to Islam, which was not born till 623 C.E., much later than even circa 604 in the second, if the Gospel of St. Barnabas was "condemned in the Gelasian Decree", which is itself of the late sixth century (or thereabout), then the following article under the entry "Barnabas Gospel of ", in the Oxford Dictionary of the Christian Church is an obvious Christian invention. The article reads:

---

49. *The Encyclopaedia Britannica*, under the heading Apocryphal Literature.

A writing in Italian, *apparently* forged, not earlier than the 15th Century by a native of Italy who had renounced Christianity for Islam. (Italics mine).

How can a document, which had, as has been shown above, been condemned before Islam was born, be forged by a Muslim convert nine hundred years later, in the fifteenth century? Condemned, too, by a Saint, who significantly "confirmed the estrangement between the Eastern and Western Churches" — in plainer words, *advanced the Pauline cause of Gentilism. The Encyclopaedia Britannica* describes "their FORGER" as a "RENEGADE" from Christianity. The virus of these two words alone would be tell-tale. The truth seems to be that as the Unitarian Gospel of Barnabas did not suit the Trinitarian Christian creed adopted at the Council of Nicaea (325 C.E.) and confirmed at the Council of Constantinople (381 C.E.) the Gospel has been given a "bad" name and "hanged" first in the Decree of Gelasius in the sixth century, and then, not content with even this, its writer dubbed a "renegade" and a "Forger", a convenient Peg on which to hang its authorship. That St. Barnabas did write a Gospel is admitted by Christian Chroniclers; e.g. in John Toland's "Nazarenus (1718) or on, Jewish, Gentile and Mahometan Christianity, containing the history of *the ancient Gospel of Barnabas*, and the modern Gospel of the Mohametans, attributed to the same apostle". (Italics mine). If the only one actually available in the world today is apparently a forgery of the fifteenth century then where is the one *really* written by St. Barnabas, the "ancient" one — and mind you, condemned not later than the sixth century? "Lo" after the usual pattern, via "condemnation"? Quite obviously, Christendom, whose disregard of history is now too well known to critical scholarship, could not stomach the truth stated in Barnabas' Gospel (the same as stated in the Qur'an, that Jesus was not crucified), and therefore brought the same disregard of history to bear on this Gospel as well.

Another significant fact is that Barnabas who had introduced the erstwhile unknown Paul to the twelve, later fell out with this same Paul. Says the Oxford Dictionary of the Christian Church: Owing to a dispute with St. Paul over John Mark; they parted as under one from the other and

Barnabas sailed for Cyprus."[50]   "When", says *The Encyclopaedia Britannica* "Barnabas sails away with Mark to resume
work in Cyprus, the mists of history close about him." The
mists of history indeed!   They *had* to chose about the too
candid Barnabas after his falling foul of a stalwart like Paul!
Quite obviously, Paul had to get rid of a man as clever as
Barnabas, not only   because the later preached truth which
clashed with Paul's brilliant heresies, but also because Paul
could not afford to have an outstanding. rival. So the greater
genius, but perhaps the lesser, and in any case the less
pugnacious, personality was gradually given a somewhat
indecent   quietus — his Gospel was first condemned, then
"forged", and finally "lost".   And, anyway, who mentions
him in Christendom today, but an old reference book or a
rebel against the priestly prevarication like Renan. Is it no
not suprising that the Christian mists of history have closed
about the disciple who was so outstanding that the Twleve
had, in the words of Renan, "attached him very closely to
themselves" and called him the Son of Consolation —
"Barnabas".[51]

Dealing with Truth, which is generally not allowed to
interfere with the convenience of Christian apologists, is
notwithstanding this, quite an embarrassing, if a passing,
ordeal to some. George Sale is one of these though even he
complacently feels that he comes out of it unscathed! Let us
see how this professedly fair-minded scholar entangles himself into a series of complications by a mental struggle between truth and partisanship. In his Preface, "To the Reader"
he says:

"..... of the Gospel of Barnabas (which I had not seen
when the little I have said of it in the Preliminary Discourse,[52] and the extract I had borrowed from Mr. de
La Monnoye and Mr. Toland,[53] were printed off), I
must beg leave to give some further account.

---

50. Acts.
51. *Ibid*.
52. Footnote, Sect. IV, p. 24.
53. In not. ad Cap. iii, p. 43.

The book is a moderate quarto, in Spanish, written in a very legible hand, but a little damaged towards the latter end. It contains two hundred and twenty-two chapters of unequal length, and four hundred and twenty pages— and is said, in the front, to be translated from the Italian, by an Arragonian; Moslem, named Mostafa de Aranda. There is a preface prefixed to it wherein the discoverer of the original MS., who was a Christian monk, called Fra-Marino, tells us, that having accidently met with a writing of Irenaeus (among others), wherein he speaks against St. Paul, alleging, for his authority, the Gospel; and that God, of His mercy, having made him very intimate with Pope Sextus V, one day, as they were together in that Pope's library, his Holiness fell asleep, and he, to employ himself, reaching down a book to read, the first he laid his hand on proved to be the very Gospel he wanted; overjoyed at the discovery, he scrupled not to hide his prize in his sleeve; and, on the Pope's awaking, took leave of him, carrying with him that celestial treasure, by reading of which he became a convert to Muhammadanism." (Footnote 6; Wect. IV, p. 24, 7. In not. ad. cap. iii, p. 43).

Incidentally, Irenaeus (C. 130—C, 200) was, like Barnabas, a Monotheist (albeit in the Christian sense), and therefore naturally opposed to a Trinitarian like Paul, who had, it must not be forgotten, fallen out with his benefactor Barnabas. Thus, the story of the Christian Monk, Fra-Marino — who "became convert to Muhammedanism", after having accidentally met with a writing of Irenaeus (among others) wherein he speaks against St. Paul, alleging, for his authority, the Gospel of St. Barnabas" — seems to ring true.

However, let us see what Sale said about this Gospel in his "Preliminary Discourse" before he had actually seen its manuscript as mentioned in his Preface, "to the Reader." On page 98 of his "Discourse" he says, "the book appears to be *no original forgery* of the "Muhammedans" though they have no doubt interpolated and altered it *since......*" After admitting that the book is no original forgery of the "Muhammedans", he says that in this book "the history of Jesus Christ is related in a manner *very different* from what we find in "true Gospels". (Italics mine) Note the mutual contradiction of these two (Italicized) statements and how, in his embarrassment, he is all the time struggling to shield himself with the implication that Barnabas's Gospel is *false* (by calling the other "true"), even after admitting that it is no forgery. But we could reasonably be asked to excuse him, as he had himself not by then seen the Gospel but only relied on the extract he "had borrowed from Mr. de la Monnoye and Mr. Toland". Let us therefore see what he says *after* he had seen the book. Says he in the later Preface, "To the Reader".

"This Gospel of Barnabas contains a complete history of Jesus Christ, from his birth to his ascension, and most of the circumstances in the four Gospels are to be found therein; but many of them turned, and some of them artfully enough, to favour the Mohammedan system. (How could "many" have been changed when "most" were as "in the four real Gospels".?) However, from the design of the whole, and the frequent interpolations of stories and passage wherein Mohammed is spoken of, and foretold by name, as the messenger of God, and the great Prophet who was to perfect the dispensation of Jesus, *It appears to be a most barefaced forgery.* (Italics mine).

Note again the mutual contradiction of the two portions in Italics, but this time the contradiction is inverted, in his earlier "Discourse"he had said that though the authenticity of the book was, so to speak, all right, the history of Jesus Christ was all wrong, i.e. different from that in the "True Gospels, Now, after seeing the Gospel, he says that though the history is all right, i.e. the same is in the "four real" Gospels, the Gospel is all wrong, i.e. a "barefaced forgery". Obviously he is ill at ease!

Also note that the Gospel of Barnabas "appears to be a most barefaced forgery " merely because in it Mohammed is .... foretold by name, and not because of any rational criticism, or historical lacuna. For instance, what if a history student called the *other* four Gospels as forgeries by Paul, who had fallen out with Barnabas and thus disregarded his Gospel? What if this disregarded and therefore "LOST" Gospel was the only one that escaped the heretical hands of Paul who changed every other record to suit his ideas of the supposedly crucified and in any case supposedly risen Christ?

78

(Witness Robert Graves's remarks on Paul in the Nazarene
Gospel Restored — "All things to all Men"[54] — The falsifying
of Jesus's own doctrine by the publication of tendentious
Greek Gospels now began — ") Either side would thus have
to be proved, and all I want to say here is that Sale's dictum
that Barnabas' Gosepl is a forgery is a statement without
support, obviously because of the tone and contradiction of
his remarks, made out of prejudice and pique, pontifically
and not rationally or critically.

But need a serious student of religious history dwell on
the writings of a man who, after exhorting his fellow
Christians that "we must not give them (Muhammedans)
ill words neither; but must avoid all reproachful language,
all that is sarcastical and biting "and , further, after saying,"
I have not, in speaking of Muhammed or his Koran, allowed
myself to use those opprobious   appellations, and
unmannerly expressions, which seem to be the strongest
arguments of several who have written against them. On the
contrary, I have thought myself obliged to treat both with
common decency...." proceeds to pour forth the vials of his
vitriolic vituperation and abuse on the Qur'an and the
Founder of Islam — throughout his "To the Reader" and his
lengthy "Preliminary Discourse". To give only a few
examples of his boasted "common decency" — he begins by
calling the Holy Book of Islam as a "manifest forgery" of
the Prophet of Islam, he says, "for how criminal soever
Muhammed may have been in imposing a false religion on
mankind..." he cannot do otherwise than applaud the
candour of the pious and learned Spanhemius; who, though
he owned him (Mohammed) to have been a wicked
imposter..."

In the face of this shameless and scurrilous invective, I can
only leave it to the imagination of the reader what the
opprobrious appellations, and unmannerly expressions of the
"several" others might have been!

And yet this is the man who has the brazenness to say
that "his (Mohammed's) great misfortune was not having
a competent knowledge of the real and pure doctrine of the
Christian   religion."   The   question of   questions is:

---

54. *The Nazarene Gospel Restored* by Robert Graves.

What is that "pure doctrine" and *where* is it? In what Christian record? In what history book in Christendom, even if one was prepared to make all the allowances for all kinds of Christian interpolation and interpretation? Even so, is it Unitarianism? Millenarianism? Arianism? Donatism? Socriniassism? Mariamism? Montanism? Quartodecimanism? Monophysitism? Nestorianism? Apollinarianism? Subordinationism? Consubstantialism? Homoousianism? Homoiousianism? Deism? Nicene Creed? Orthodox Creed? Roman Catholicism? Protestantism?" So on, and so on, and so on?.... "In 1900 the U.S. had no fewer than 250 different kinds of Christianity."[55]

Incidentally, I understand that there is a Clarendon Press (Oxford) edition of 1907 of the Gospel of Barnabas in the British Museum which has these words on the title page: "The Gospel of Barnabas edited and translated from the Italian MS. In the Imperial Library of Vienna, by Lonsdale and Laura Ragg with a facsimile". These words are at least silent on the point of any forged authorship, and silence on something so hurting to Christendom as this "forgery", is significantly suggestive that the "forgery" itself may have been forged!

Now about the destruction of unwanted records. This is amply proved by Christian methods in the earlier centuries. "The Church", says Mr. Archibald Robertson in The *Humanist* (London, November 1958); took good care of that, after Christianity became the religion of the Empire, the Christian writings of Prophry and others systematically hunted out and burnt, so we know very little about them. We are left with the *obiter dicta* of Pliny, Tacitus, Suetonius, Lucian, and Marcus Aurelius, and with quotations from Celsus which occur in Origen's reply and which the Church negligently forgot to censor.

Theologians whose views were not, for instance, Trinitarian, or who were Millenarians (believing in the Physical Kingdom of God lasting only a thousand years "during which He — Christ — will reign upon earth in a kingdom of His saints and at its conclusion take them with Him into heaven," or who were in respect in disagreement

---

55. *Times*, 26 May, 1961.

with the decrees of the Council of Nicaea and Constantinople (in other words, Arians and others whose creed did not conform to the Nicene Creed), were doomed. Their works were first condemned then destroyed, and then, conveniently, declared "lost". Examples abound; only a few, picked up a random, are quoted from *The Oxford Dictionary of the Christian Church*. No comments are needed except that I have put the significant portions in Italics:

(1) *Prophyry* (C. 232—303) "........ of more lasting significance was his treatise in fifteen books against the Christians, it was condemned *to be burnt* in 448......."

(2) *Victorinus*, St. (d.c. 304) "'.......... was the first exegete of the W. Church, *but nearly all his works are lost, probably on account of his millenarianist tendencies,* which caused them to be *condemned* as apocryphal by the Decretum Galasianum........"

(3) *Apollinarius and Apollinarianism.* Apollinarius or Apollinarius the younger (C. 310—c. 390) "....... Teaching akin to that of Apollinarius was *condemned* at the Council of Alexandria in 362 C., but soon afterwards he explained himself satisfactorily. His characteristic christological teaching, which was little known before 371, was explicity condemned by Synods at Rome in 374—380 and by the Council of Constantinople of 381 the State forbade Apollinarian public worship. Of his many works only *fragments remain....*" Of Apollinarius's extensive writings most have been lost....." "But"— (and this in significant) "— fragments of his....... apologetic works *against prophyry (in 30 books) and the Exp.* Julian (i.e. Julian the "Apostate)" have...... *been preserved"*! *the same Prophyry, that is, whose* anti-Christian works had been *"condemned to be burnt."*

(4) *Lucian of Antioch, St.* (d. 312) "....... he founded an influential theological school of which both Arius and Eusebius of Nicomedia were members; indeed his subordinationist teaching seems to have been the immediate source of

Arian heresy. Only a few fragments of his writings have survived." Subordinationism is defined in the Dictionary thus: A *heretical* form of Trinitarian teaching which regards either the Son as subordinate to the Father or the Holy Ghost as subordinate to both.

(5) *Arius* (C. 25—C. 336) "... accordingly an Oecumenical Council met at Nicaea in 325, and ... condemned to be burnt "Arius..." Arius seems to have *written little.* He embodied his doctrine (the Principle of Divinity of Jesus Christ) in popular songs" of which *only fragments survive*"

(6) *Nestorianism* "... in 435 Nestorius was banished to upper Egypt where he died several years later. "Nestorius's principal writings were his letters and sermons, which, however, for the most part, survive only in fragments."

(7) *Origen* (C. 185—C. 254) "Origen was a very fertile author. *Many of his writings have perished and most of others survive only in fragments* or in Latin translations .... He has often been accused of teaching "Subordinationism" and, ... when Origen's *teaching was condemned* (By the way, this Origen was otherwise such a good Christian that, in an excess zeal to carry out the word of Jesus literally — mutilated himself! (Matthew: xix. 12).

An interesting sidelight on the descturction of unwanted records is thrown by the following from J. R. Dore's Old Bibles, 1868 edition (page 26, Tyndale's first edition of the New Testament of: 525).

The English Bishops carefully examined Tyndale's translation and, instead of making a better one, as they ought to have done, endeavoured to suppress it.

They had the greatest reverence for what Tunstall calls "the most holy word of God", and considered Luther's testament (from which Tyndale is said to have translated his) to be a profanation of it, *they therefore feel it their duty to destroy every copy they could obtain.*

Whilst we condemn the burning of Tyndale's work we do not forget that it *was the custom of the age to burn the works of opponents,* as Luther a few years before burnt the books of the Canon Law and the bull of Pope Leo, outside the walls of Wittenberg, and in 1552, John Calvin burnt all the copies he could collect of Servetus's Bible, at Geneva, *because they contained some notes he did not think to be orthodox.* (Italics mine).

Would it surprise anyone after this to hear Joseph McCabe say?

Libraries of from 100,000 to 700,000 books existed in the Greco-Roman cities until the fifth century, preserving all that the race had won in science, philosophy, and history. *They were all destroyed by the Christians.* The largest of them all, *that of Alexandria, was destroyed by the same monks and nobles who murdered Hypatia: for the story, that this library was burnt three* centuries later by the Arabs is a very late and now discredited fiction. (Italics mine).

Burning, by the way, was a pastime with the Christian Priests, not only indulged in regarding records, but regarding humans, who, when they did not conform, were burnt alive. The stake is almost an exclusive Christian symbol of torture for propagating the love-message of the Prince of Peace!

Is it any wonder, therefore, that St. Barnabas's Gospel has been "lost", and the one that is available is a "forgery", and by a "renegade"? Mercifully enough, the usual Christian audacity in this respect is hedged in by the word "apparently" — "apparently a forgery". But this could not perhaps be helped inconveniently, a Gospel according to Barnabas does exist!

The Gospel of St. Barnabas was written after the date of the Ascension of Jesus, according to the "A History of the Christian Church".[56] The earliest designation of a passage from the Gospels as scripture was about C. 131, by the so-called Barnabas." — Synoptic and St. John even in the second century. Would it, therefore, be any wonder, human nature being what it is, if memory made room for wishfulness, exactly proportionate to the acknowledged ignorance of the inheritors of the tradition on the one hand, and to the cunning and greed of the interlopers and exploiters on the other?

---

56. Barn., 4. quoted in *"A History of the Christian"*, by Williston Wolker, Professor of Ecclesistical History in Yale University, p. 62

Human hands replace the Divine Hand. Things made by God cannot be replaced by man made things. The Divine revelation given to Jesus having lost its purity is here for all to see for themselves. On this point a non-Muslim writer Muir, in his book *Life of Muhammad*, states as follows:

"The Christianity of the seventh century was itself decrepit and corrupt. It was disabled by contending schisms, and had substituted the puerilities of superstition for the pure expansive faith of early ages."

Joseph Lawins in his book *The Bible Unmasked* (Free thought Association, new York, 1928) has also bitterly criticised current Christianity for having incorporated almost all popular Pagan precepts and practices and then destroyed all such pagan records and libraries in order to obliterate the origin of the flesh so alien to Jesus. Similarly, Joseph Wheless, in the *Forgery in Christianity*, has thoroughly exposed the whole of Christianity as the hand work of misguided priests. At one place he says:

"Truely and prophetically spoke Zola that civilisation will not attain to its perfection until the last stone from the Past Church falls cn the last priest."

The evidence that the Church, as built by the Priests of the dark medieval days, owes everything to the Pagan world, and not to the sacred name under which it passes, is so overwhelmingly preponderating in nature that one becomes compelled to say with full justification, in the words of the Archbishop of York, that the Church repels. If the laity has realised that in their worship in the church they are only worshipping myth and superstition propounded by Paul and the like, and keeping up the tradition of the Pagaon cult, will they not resent it?

No wonder the pews have become empty benches. The situation has become serious; the Church religion is at its lowest ebb, and the Archbishop of Canterbury is thinking of means to keep "the strayed flock within the pale". As early as 1923 Dr. Simpson, in the Church Congress held at Plymouth, remarked that where there were ten people who come to church before the war, five perhaps came now: "In the country Christianity is fighting for its existence, and losing ground steadily. The churches no longer influence modern Englishmen; and with the spread of education, they are being deserted by the women."

This inattentiveness to religion in the West has perturbed many minds, which set themselves to search for some satisfactory explanation. And the knot was entangled by the candid remarks that the church as it exists today does not teach the religion needed by man.

As Archibald Hamilton so aptly said:

"Whereas Islam guides humanity in the daily work day life, the present day so called Christianity, indirectly in theory and invariably in practice, teaches its followers, it would seem, to pray to God on Sundays and to prey on His creation for the rest of the week."

James Isa A. Okeke says:

"Christianity is unreal to humanity, being only a system of theology which ignores the secular needs of life; that Christ was not the author of Christianity, soon the Christendom will come to realise it."

An enlightened or enquiring mind falls to get a rational explanation of the Christian dogmas relating to Trinity, Divinity of Christ, Divine Sonship, Original Sin and Atonement, Dualism between matter and spirit, infallibility of Pope, the institution of Nuns, the nature of Gospels and many other confusing and conflicting issues which have become part and parcel of Christianity with the result that it could not hold its own against the onslaughts of reason and its building started crumbling like a house of cards.

I am sorely grieved to remark here that the majority of Christian missionaries and clergies, instead of attacking and vilifying the pure and perfect principles of Islam, ought to impart life and spirituality to their own dying creed. Nevertheless, they are so bent upon this course as if it were the aims and end of the religion they teach. They should first attend to humanity. It has undergone such a complete metamorphoris and is so changed that if Jesus himself were to come back, he would simply shudder at the very sight of present day Christianity.

THE WRITERS OF THE FOUR GOSPELS

We are, hereunder, presenting a short story of the four Gospels which will light on the way they came into being: At the General Council of Nicaea held in the year 325 C.E., where two thousand and forty eight bishops assembled to decide theological matters and also to select, those books from out of a vast collection of manuscripts which, in their judgement, constituted the authorised word of God, under the chairmanship of Emperor Constantine. The meeting started with a great deal of enthusiasm. Everyone of the bishops tried to see that his own predetermined concept prevailed. Emperor Constantine used his Imperial authority and disqualified seventeen hundred and thirty bishops from having a voice in deciding which books were or were not to be selected as the word of God. This step dampened the spirit of the remaining bishops whom Emperor Constantine chose not to disqualify on consideration of their being in agreement with the preconceived ideas of their sovereign.

Thomas Paine, in his book *Age of Reason*, says the Councils of Nicaea and Laodicea were held about 350 years after the time of Christ is said to have lived; and the books that now compose the New Testament were then voted for by YEAS and NAYS, as we now vote a law. A great many that were offered had a majority of NAYS, and were rejected. This is the way the New Testament Come into being.(*Age of Reason*, p. 92).

Out of some fifty Gospels, only those of Matthew, Mark, Luke and John were selected and rest were burned. The Emperor then decreed that the above decision be considered as sanctioned by the Divine Will and that the mentioned four Gospels should be implicitly believed as the word of God. He then ordered that the rejected manuscripts be burned and that anyone found to be possessing, concealing or otherwise preaching anything other than the authorised word of God should be punished with death. All Bishops bowed down before the power of His Imperial Majesty-Constantine. Constantine, therefore, produced the first copy of the New Testament.

(1) The Gospels of Matthew, Mark and Luke are called synoptic Gospels because of their similarity and form. Of these Mark's is the very first. St. Mark was the interpreter and an attendant of apostle Peter. Eusebius in his Church History, says "Mark having become the interpreter of Peter, wrote down accurately whatever things he remembered of the things said or done by Jesus Christ. For he neither heard the Lord nor followed him, but afterwards as I said, he followed Peter, and was a relative of Barnabas

(Co. 1.4:10).

Ancient tradition certifies the Mark was a true companion of Peter. The book is called Peter's Gospel by some very ancient writers. However, it is generally conceded that Peter may have furnished, or suggested, much of the material found in the book. Peter, we are told, denied and cursed 'Jesus three times and Jewish Elders labelled him as unlearned and ignorant". (Acts. 4:13).

(2) Next to be written was Matthew. Matthew (also called Levi) was one of twelve apostles, (Mk. 2:14) undoubtedly a jew who was a Publican, or Roman tax collector,(Ch.10:3).

Black's Bible Dictionary says that the Gospel does not impress the reader as being the account of an eye witness, Besides, the fact it was written in Greek, (as held by the Editor of the New Analytical Bible) and that it is based on a variety of Greek sources makes it difficult to believe that its author was one of the original disciples. The expression of the Jewish view point suggests that it must have been written by one of the Paulist Christian Jews.

The Oxford revised Edition of the Bible says, "this Gospel is anonymous. The unknown Christian teacher who prepared it during the last third of the first century may have used as one of his sources a collection of Jesus' sayings that apostle Matthew is said to have made.

(3) Now, we come to Luke, the beloved Physician, see Col. 4:14. Reputed author of Luke and Acts, both books being addressed to his patron Theophilus.

Luke was a close friend and travelling companion of Paul, as is shown in his personal allusions recording the journeys of the apostle. See in the book of Acts where the author changes the pronouns to "we" and "us" indicating that he himself was present at these times, Acts, 16:10; 20:6; 27:1; 28:16.

Many students see something of the stamp of Paul's doctrine in Luke's Gospel. The exact date of the writing of the Gospel is unknown. But if it were written after Luke came under Paul's influence, it would be quite natural that the latter should give some coloring to the narrative."

(The New Chain — Reference Bible p. 208).

Luke never saw Jesus nor did he hear him. The man who neither saw nor heard Jesus, and who wrote from memory of what he heard from people other than Jesus and who earned eloquent praise from Paul cannot repeat the word of God. He wrote only what his own wisdom or writing ability could produce under the influence of others and according to Paul's teaching.

However, all this lead us to the conclusion that three synoptic Gospels do seem to have a common source commonly called the "Q" (Quello or Source) which however does not exist. In any case the three gospels contain the word of man and not of God indeed.

(4) The Gospel of John is the fourth Gospel in the New Testament. It is considered by many to be the most deepest book in the Bible.

The Acts of the Apostle says that Peter and John, were unlearned and ignorant men. (Acts, 4:13), if there be any truth in the words contained in the Acts then it is impossible to imagine an "unlearned and ignorant John writing the Gospel ascribed to him. The Gospel of John is not a mere repetition of a tale or a description of some incident, it is a drama whose successive scenes reveal the glory of Christ in a very masterly fashion. The author of this beautiful piece of writing must have been some very great writer, about whom we know nothing.

Commenting on the Gospel of John, William Neil writes, "This Gospel presents many difficult problems of interpretation, primarily as to how far it may be regarded an accurate record of the words and deeds of Jesus. The general view would be that this is not so much an attempt to give a photographic reproduction of the life and teaching of Jesus, as to draw out the significance of what Jesus said and did, again with a view to showing the wider non-Jewish world the importance of what had recently happened in Palestine. It is rather the product of reflection on what Jesus meant than accurate reportage". (The *Rediscovery of Bible*, pp. 80,81).

Black's Bible Dictionary supporting the view that apostle John did not write this Gospel lists following argument:

(a) The appendix (chapter 21) in endorsing the Gospel does not claim John the apostle was its writer.

(b) The Gospels and the Acts show John as of a fiery temperament, ambitious to be the first in the Kingdom and an adherent of Jewish party in the Church. The spirit of love pervading this Gospel and its bias against the Jewish point of view argue against such an author.

(c) John was beheaded before 70 C.E. hence no connection with Ephesius can be established.

(d) The great doctrine of LOGOS borrowed from Greek Philosophy provides conclusive proof that John the apostle was not the author.

Jesus A Live Christ

"In our survey we have noticed that the Gospels are essentially a production of the Church which, in turn, is the product of Paul's penetrating intelligence. Irrespective of the consideration who wrote what, the fact remains that the NT is the collection of books whose author was directly or indirectly Paul, the crafty Jew".

Paul and real Apostles of Jesus were no friends.

PSEUDO-AUTHORS OF CANONICAL GOSPELS
Are the Canonical Gospels Written on the base of Travel Pattern of Jesus?

In the C.S.C. No. 9. Drs. Jan Slomp states that "The Canonical Gospels are based on the travel Pattern of Jesus. (Page 125). This, claim should not be misled by his 'historical blunders'. The following may be borne in mind for enlightment.

Professor J. Volckart, S.J., of Sacred Scripture, says that "It is evident we should not expect the sayings of Our Lord to be reproduced word for word,..........we should not expect a miraculous reproduction of the exact words of Our Divine Savour, moreover, we have not the words of Our Lord as He spoke them in His mother-tongue".

(The Saviour, Introduction, page 9).

The Christian Scholars admit that Mark and Luke were neither the disciples of Jesus nor were they eye-witnesses. Of course Matthew and John were "called" by Jesus. There is much controversy as to the authorship, late and even as to whether it were all written by the same person, which they ascribed to them or it were written by others (PSEUDO) under their names!

St. MARK

"Marcus (Markus), Roman name of John Mark, a kinsman of Barnabas, when he is a fellow worker with Paul (Philem. 24). He was recommended by the apostle to church at closse (col. 4:10). That John Mark had fully reinstated himself with Paul is shown by the latter's statement in Timothy 4:11:- "Take Mark, and bring him with thee; for he is useful to me for ministering". (New Corupact Dicationary 344).

He was interpreter and disciple of Peter—the longtime follower of Peter and when Peter after outbreak of the Ncronian Persecution, wrote his circular letter to the Christians of Asia Minor the only name (apart from that of Silvanus or Silas) is the name of "Marcus my Son".

(1 Peter 5:13).

"The Phrase implies at once a disparity of not less then fifteen or twenty years in age and special bond of long and affectionate relationship. Where are we to find room for this intercourse, and what exactly is menat by the word interpreter?"

Luke

A student of Paul — he did not see Jesus. He wrote his version of Gospel while in Caeseria in Greek language after fifty six or fifty eight years under inspiration.

John

He was a disciple of Jesus. He wrote his version of Gospel at Ephesu or in its vicinity. It is in the Greek language. It was written about ninety eight or one hundred and twenty years, after Jesus though he was one of the early desciples of Jesus.

The rest of the twenty three Epistles were written in Greek languages in Rome and Greece also under inspiration. Only two of the Epistles were written in Jerusalem or Palestine. They date between fifty to fifty eight years after Christ.

History proves that the version different version of Gospel were written between forty one and ninety eight years after Christ. It may be 'kept in mind that the epistles of Pausl were written before the Gospel. It was probably during his first stay in Corinth about the year 51 A.D. that Paul began writing his letters or Epistles. These unique literary treasurers, now part of the New Testament, constitute Christinaity's earliest record. The Gospel had yet to be published when Paul composed them in Greek addressed to the young Churches or to individuals.

The letters of Paul are, however, most unexplicable without Gospel. The earliest Gospels were three; called the Synoptic, the Matthew, Mark and Luke. But as the Gospel of John was written after ninety eight years, it is difficult to know when it was joined with the three earlier Gospels. History is silent in this respect; moreover, it was also difficult to prove that the Gospel known to be written by John was actually written by him. It is perhaps because of this that the Gospels are regarded and claimed to be written under divine inspiration — for this belief gives the Gospel the status of an Holy record safe from alterations, and not as a mere historic record which may be subjected to errors.

The writers themselves had claimed it to have been written by them under inspiration. (Matt. 10:20). "He will teach you everything (J. 14:26)

ST. MATTHEW

1. What do we mean by 'according to St. Matthew'? Not necessarily that St. Matthew was the author of the book; though, when the title was first added to the Gospel, he was probably believed to be thus. No where do we find the marks of the eyewitness as we find them in Mark and John. For the narrative the writer is generally dependent upon Mark, and seems nowhere to introduce reminiscences of his own; while the incidents, which he, adds, do not suggest apostolic authorship. But we can hardly suppose that St. Matthew had nothing to do with the Gospel; had the title been a pure invention, we should have found the name of a more prominent Apostle. It is here that papias (Eus. H.E., iii, 39) comes to our aid. "Matthew", he tells us, "Composed the Logia in Hebrew, and everyone interpreted them as he was able". Now the word "Logia" often translated 'Oracles' suggests discourse rather than incidents; and much is explained' if we suppose that it is to St. Matthew that we chiefly owe that lost Christian document, to which modern scholars refer as Q (cf. The Synoptic Problem, 38 pp). If Papias is referring to the Gospel as we here it today, he is certainly in error. Matthew is based on the Greek Gospel of Mark, and a Greek Q is presupposed by the strange Greek forms reproduced alike by Matthew and Luke. (cf. Mk. 11:11; Luk 7:28, Mt. 8:8, Lk. 7:6,7) What St. Matthew probably wrote, was a Hebrew or Aramaic account of the Lords' teaching similar to that part of the book of Isiah

which is concerned with Isiah of Jerusalem. It consisted
for the most part of discourses, and said nothing of the
passion or Resurrection. But it related our Lord's Call and
Temptation; and it gave short narratives, like those of Is 7
and 8, when they were necessary for the understanding of His
words (cf. Mt. 11:2.6) Matthew was probably were generally
men with a past (Lk.15:14,15) and the Custom-house of
Capernaum was a very important one. Probably also he
was, of all the Apostles, the most accustomed to the use of
the pen; and he may, like euclides in the Theactetus of
Plato (143) have written, down many of the Master's words
during that Master's lifetime. If, as is almost certain, it is
the Gospel according to St. Matthew which gives us more
fully than anyother the contents of Q, it is Q which is the
most important element in it, and there was but little error
in attaching to it the Apostle's name. But the actual author
is a compiler rather than an original authority, and he does
not claim, as even St. Luke does, to be more than this".

(*A New Commentary on Holy Scripture* by
Charles Gore, P. 125, Published S.P.C.K.London, 1937).

2. Under such circumstances it would seem most natural to
assume that the Gospel, like the Gospel of Matthew, was
written by one who was not himself a personal disciple of
Christ and an eyewitness of the events which he records,
but was possessed of sources of the first rank; so that his
account so far as it is based on his sources, but unreliable
in other parts."

(*A History of Christianity in the Apstolic Age*
by Arthur Cushman McGiffert, Ph.,D.D.D., p.613).

PSEUDO-MATTHEW

"This Gospel, which is attributed by tradition to
Matthew (P. Levi), is perhaps, in its present form the second
of the Synoptic records.

The earliest indirect mention of such a work by
Matthew is that of Papias of Hierapolis (early second
century), " a hearer of John", who wrote a book, An
Exposition of the Oracles of the Lord', extracts from which

are preserved by Eusebius and Irenaeus. The former writer says (H.E. iii. 39) "Matthew compiled the Oracles in the Hebrew (= Aramaic) dialect, and every one interpreted them as he was able."

It is uncertain, however, as to precisely what is meant by "Oracles": and Collections of the "Sayings' (Logia) of Jesus may be referred to rather than the Gospel.

The Oldest direct witness to Matthaean authorship is found in a fragment of the works of Apollinaris of Hierapolis (180 A.D.), who says that the Quartodecimans appealed to Matthew for the view of the Paschal Supper being held on the 14th of Nisan.[57]

The problems of the authorship and origin of this Gospel is also much complicated by the question of its relationship to author's works, The Gospel according to the Hebrew.[58] Opinions are much divided, but the balance, perhaps, inclines to our present Gospel being largly a trnaslation of some Aramaic document now lost.[59]

The question of the date of the original Gospel is also a matter of doubt, but the most probable estimate fixes it at about 70 A.D., just after the time of the destruction of Jerusalem, though some extreme critics have dated it subsequently to 100 A.D. Any Aramaic text, if such ever existed, must have been an earlier work.

The sources of the internal contents of the Gospel have also been a matter of dispute. Some critics advocate a primitive ORAL GOSPEL, others assert the sources to be largely documentary. For the purpose of our inquiry Matthew, in its present forms, may be regarded as separable into the following constituent parts:

1. Marcan traditions of missionary journeys.
2. Ancient LOGIA (?Aramaic) specially edited by the author.
3. Various supplementary Historical and Traditional Narratives inserted in the work, e.g.:
   (a) Genealogical Table.
   (b) Birth and Infancy Stories (?Palestinian)
   (c) Additional episodes, e.g. story of the death of Judas, Appearances of the dead at crucifixion. Apostle's Commission etc."(Must be written by Psedo Matthew).

57. *Chron.Pasc. Alex.*, ed. Bonn, vol. 1, p. 14.
58. *Jerome*, De Vir, iii., C. 2.
59. See etc, *Originals prechodes Matthew Evangel*, p. 115 f. *Black beitrage Sur Evangelien. Kritik*, pp. 57,58. Also art "*Matthew Hasting's Diet, of Bib.*

Pseudo Matthew).

Of these sections, however, we are only concerned with two:

The Genealogical Table, and

The Birth Story;

and the questions with which a criticism of the evidence of Matthew as to the subject of the Virgin Birth has to deal may be stated thus (1) what is the ORIGIN and VALUE of the Genealogy, and (2) what are the Probable ORIGINAL READINGS and MEANING of verses 16, 18, 20 and 25, of Chapter L

(1) The Genealogy[60] professes to show the lineal descent of Jesus from Abraham through David. And the whole family tree is divided into three sections, viz:

"Abraham to David, 14 generations; David until the carrying away into Babylon, 14 generations; and from the carrying away into Babylon unto Christ 14 generations; in all, 42 generations.

Now it is probable that the first thing which strikes the modern reader is the extreme artificiality of arrangement in this document. We have, in fact, three courses of exactly $7 \times 2 = 14$ names in each section. On comparing this list with the similar geneaology given in Luke iii, we find great discrepancies.[61] The latter writer inverts the order of succession, and traces the line beyond Abraham. Also there are variations in the names and number of the generations. Luke 17 generations between Joseph and Zerubbable, Matthew 9. Most of the names also differ, and in verse 8 of Matthews list three names are omitted — an arrangement apparently intentional in order to preserve numerical symmetry.[62]

Another question arises, whence were these documents obtained? In answer to this it has been suggested that they perhaps were part of the temple records, compiled and kept by the Priest.[63]

---

60. See Deut. xxvii: 2—8; Same. xxii:24; P.hil. 111:5, and Josephus, Life, I., for ref. to similar documents.

61. See Wiesler, Achran, Synop, of the Gospels, ed. Venables (1878), and Lord A. Hervey's The Genealogy of Qur Lord (1853) for attempts reconciliation.

62. Cp I Chron iii: 11, 12.

63. Academy, Dec. 8, 1894

There is nothing intrinsically improbable in a such theory, and since such records are known to have been officially kept, this Genealogy in question may have been so derived.

But there is evidence to show that these official records were not unfrequently "manipulated", and made to subserve the purposes of "rabbinical subleties" of exegesis from time to time. It is clear, therefore, that such tables, whatever may have been original value from an historic point of view, from the various alterations that may have been made of deliberate intent, and the errors that probably crept in during transcriptions, cannot now be regarded as strictly accurate and reliable documents in the modern sense of the term.

With reg..rd † the original readings of verses 76 and 18, and their authenticity and value in conjunction with those of 19 and 20, we have a problems of great difficulty and complexity. We will, in considering this, take as the basis of our examination the readings adopted by a modern critical Textus Receptus". In this, verse 16 reads:

"And Jacob begot Joseph, the husband of Mary, from whom was begotten Jesus, who is called Christ".

Here we have, as a result of the collation of the best MSS., a statement that Jesus was "begotten" of Mary, but no direct reference to the question of paternity, which is distinctly stated in the case of every other in the Genealogy This omission however, is supplied in verses 18 and 20, where the paternity of Jesus is ascribed to the Holy Ghost, and we read:

"When his mother was espoused to Joseph, before they came together, she was found with Child of the Holy Spirit.... Joseph, thou son of David, fear not to take unto thee Mary thy wife, for that which is conceieved in her is of the Holy Spirit'.

This reading of verse 16 was, in general, accepted as the most probable one until the discovery in 1892, in a Monastery on Mount Sinai, by Mrs. A. S. Lewis of a Syriac Palimpsest MS. of the four Gospels.[6][5] In this MS. we find another and

---

64. *Academy*, Dec., 8, 1894.
65. See Harnach in Preussirche Fahribiicher, May, 1898; Nestle, all-gemeng. Also Dr. Rendel Harris in contemporary Review, Nov. 1894.

undoubtedly early reading, which gives us:

"Jacob begot Joseph; Joseph, to whom was betrothed Mary the Virgin, begot Jesus, who is called the Messiah."

Here we have apparently, at least a distinct assignment of parentage to Joseph. In the Curetonian Syriac MS.[66] the reading more nearly resembles that of the Greek codices.

The Synoptical Gospels:

Matthew wrote the Logia in the Hebrew language, and each one interpreted these as he could'. Till recent times (Eusebii, Historic Ecclesiastiea, lib,111,C.39).
(*ibid.*, p. 448).

was universally taken for granted that the two evengelic writings referred to by Papias were our canonical Matthew and Mark, the first Gospel, as we have it, being Matthew's Hebrew original done into Greek. Modern critics for the most part dissent from the traditional view, but not to the extent of treating the statements of Papias as of no account. They believe that Matthew and Mark did write books relating to the ministry of Jesus as Papias declares. With reference to Mark critics are not agreed whether the book ¹.e wrote was our canonical Gospel bearing his names are, was related to it as a first sketch to a revised edition, the ground for the doubt being that this canonical Mark seems to be a some what one sided record of the things done by Jesus, rather than a balanced account both of things done and of things said. With reference to Matthew, the prevailing opinion is that he did not write our first Gospel, but a book consisting chiefly of saying of Jesus, furnished probably with brief historical introduction, explaining the occasions on which they were uttered, though to what length the historical element extended in a matter, of disputation. These two writings, Mark's narrative and Matthew's Logia, critics regard as the two chief sources of synoptical Gospels, the former of the incidents common to the three, the latter of the sayings common to "Matthew" and "Luke". As such they form the solid foundations of the evengelic history, the guarantee that when two or three of the Synoptical Gospels

---

66. *Brought from Egypt in 1842* by Archedeacon Tattam, and edited by Dr. Curetoh.

agree in their report of what Jesus said or did we are in
contact with fact, and not fiction.   (*Ibid.*, p. 449).

(11)

BIBLE

For the millions the only means of knowing the sacred
books is through translations, which, however, faithfully
executed on the whole, do nevertheless but imperfectly
reflect the sense of the original. Then even for the learned
the Hebrew and Greek texts do not exist in their original
purity. Nay, the text of the Hebrew Bible, with which we
are at present concerned, never existed as one whole, in
absolute purity".

(*Apologetics or Christianity Defensively   Stated* by
Alexander Balmain Bruce, D.D., P. 304).

LOGOS

"The doctrine of the logos was no part of the personal
teaching of Christ. It does not belong to the evangelic
history, but to the philosophy or theological construction
of that history". (p. 469).

He (Paul) derived the one half from the school of
Gamatiel, the other from the school of Philo.

(*Ibid.*, 436).

"The Gospel and the Epistles give no indication of when
or   where they were written, and so do not help us to
discover much of his activity".

(*The Church in the New Testament* by Rev. Sebastian
Bullough, O.P.,M.A.,S.T.L. p. 225.)

"Perhaps we should add a note here that although John
at the beginning of II and III Epistles, refers to himself
as the "Ancient" or the "Presbyter", and is often so called
in the   legends, there was possibly another John the
Presbyter or Priest living at Ephesus, mentioned by Papias"
(*Ibid.*, 228.)

WHICH GOSPEL

The Gospel is the glad-tiding which Jesus and his
Apostles announced. Very soon, however, several of the

early Christians including St. Barnabas attempted to put into writing, an account of the life and words of Jesus Christ. (Luke, 1:1). Four such written accounts of the Gospel were later officially recognized by the council of Nice and were included among the Canonical Scripture; they are four verslons namely, Matthew, Mark, Luke and John (out of many) of "the Gospels". As we gather from the works of early Christians (already towards the middle of the second century), these records were, owing to their contents, soon called "gospel". The word "Gospel", then, may mean either the glad-tiding that were announced by Jesus and preached by the Apostles, or the books in which later the principal features, of the apostolic preaching, were gathered. These four little books are the biographies of Jesus Christ, they however, do not give us a full account of all deeds and saying of Jesus Christ as St . John himself declared:

"There are many other miracles Jesus did in presence of his disciples, which are not written down in this book, so much as has been written down, that you may learn to believe Jesus is the Christ". (John 20:30).

Strictly speaking, God is not the author of these Gospels, nor He acutally executed the writing Miraculously. Professor, J. Volckeert, S.J., of St. Mary's Theological College, Kursiong, writes in-the "Introduction" of the "Four Gospels, written by Fr. C. Bulcke, S.J.

"It should be noted that at times the evange =list adds to the discourse of our Lord his own Theological Interpretation. It is evident that we should not expect the saying of our Lord to be reproduced word for word ...... We should not expect a miraculous reproduction of the exact words of our divine Saviour; moreover, we have not the words of Our Lord as he spoke them in his mother tongue". (page ix).

In the New Testament, the word Gospel never means a book (one of the four Gospels) but always the good tidings which Christ announced and the apostle preached The reason why Jesus's Gospel was called glad tidings, is that it gave thegood news of the advent of the last of the Prophets, which is variously described in Jesus's metaphorical language as the advent of the Kingdom of God (Mark. 1:15), the coming of the Lord. (Mathew 21:40), the appearance of the Comforter (John 14:16) or the Spirit of Truth (John, 14:17), etc.

GOSPEL OF BARNABAS

In keeping with this point, St.Barnabas convey the 'glad-tiding' of the advent of Prophet Muhammad (peace be upon him) so as to show by this good news that God Almighty is the only Lord of the World, who is known in the ancient record as God of Abraham, or God of Jacob. Remembering the law, that the progress of Old Testament doctrine must be traced in the light of the New Testament, similarly, we can discern through the Holy Qur'an the teaching of the New Testament. The Holy Qur'an points out yet another progress, namely, that the WAY OF LIFE and RIGHTEOUSNESS is not through "faith", but through good works. Thus in Islam the good works are LIVING WORKS which manifests itself in obedience that worketh in love.

So far the purpose of the Bible is concerned, it was meant for and confined to a family of Isaac. As such its scope of guidance was limited to such an extent that even the conception of God was tribal, God was not known to be of all mankind but God of Abraham and God of Jacob, is family God.

When we compare the Gospel of Barnabas with the canonized Gospels, it becomes clear to us that the writers of the four Gospels were influenced by the Greek philosophy and were not at all inspired by God or the teachings of the prophets. They have, therefore, exerted their endeavours to place Jesus in the ranks of the Greek gods. They have, infact, presented Jesus as an incarnated god who is annoyed even like small children at slight matters and orders his disciples to be gone. He addressed Peter saying *"Be get, O Satan!"* Similarly, he is pleased at slight matters and changes the names of his disciples, hands over the keys of heaven to Peter: sometimes he assumes the character of a supernatural being and commands the winds to stop and the storms to cease. He turns the water into wine, cures the ailing and brings the dead back to life. He makes such claims which are fit only for God. But when we hear him on the cross in the last moments of his life saying *"My God my God, why hast thou forsaken me?"* (Matthev 27:46). We realise that he was only an humble servant of God, though his followers turned him into what he could never have imagined. He was neither a Greek nor was Greek his language. He could neither think like the Greek nor talk like them. Greek was really Greek to him.

In contrast to it, Barnabas presents all the real events that had taken place in the life of his Master even as the four Gospels. The Gospel of Barnabas contains life of Jesus from his birth to his ascension. It begins with the miraculous birth of Jesus and deals with his circumcision, the visit of Magy, the Massacre of Infants, the flight into and the return of the family from Egypt and discussion with Doctors in the temple. It also deals with the Jesus Ministry Period, his journeys, discourse, parables and ethical and eschatological teachings. Finally it gives a description of Paschal supper and records the betrayel, the trial and the erucifixion. The Gospel concludes with the reappearance of the Jesus and his ascension to heaven.

Apparently, the descriptions of the Gospel of Barnabas and the four Gospels seem to be similar, but there really exists a great difference. The style of the four Gospels is philosophic and even apostatic while the style of the Gospel of Barnabas is similar to that of the prophets and is in methodical arrangement. Of the four Gospels give incomplete reports while the Gospel of Barnabas gives complete reports. For example, Luke writes: "and a certain ruler asked him, saying Good Master: what shall I do to inherit eternal Life." Whereupon he said: "Why callest thou me good, none is good save one that is God" (Luke 18: 18—19). If one reads these remarks carefully, one finds them neither inspiring nor convincing but finds them rather confusing. Now read the same report in the Gospel of Barnabas and conclude for yourself which is the real Gospel! (And how) Barnabas has filled up the gaps that are to be found in the Four Gospels.

Jesus answered: "Thou callest me good, and knowest not that God alone is good, even as said Job, the friend of God; "A child of a day old is not clean; yes, even the angels are not faultless in God's presence. Moreover, he said: "The flesh attracteth sin, and sucketh up iniquity as a sponge sucketh up water."

(Barnabas, ch. LXVI, 68 b).

The Christians of the modern times claim that the four Gospels were written under inspiration by the Holy Ghost. But this claim has never been made by any of the compiler of the Gospels. So, the claim that these Gospels were written under inspiration by the Holy Ghost needs proof. It is, however, not my aim to prove that the four Gospels were not written under inspiration, what I mean is to show that the Gospel of Barnabas completes the incomplete narrations of the four Gospels (canonical) and differs from them in many basic and essential points, which are as follows:

1. Jesus never claimed himself to be the son of God: he of course denied it.
2. The son of Abraham presented for sacrifice was Ishmail.
3. The Promised Messiah was not Jesus.
   He was, in fact, Prophet Muhammad (p.b.u.h.).
4. Jesus was not crucified, he was taken up to heaven.

T' e Gospel of Barnabas, on different occasions, differs from the four Gospels in the style of narration, as it busies itself in academic and spiritual matters instead of philosophic problems. It is so because Jesus himself talked in the style of the propehts and preached his sacred teachings. His style was so simple yet impressive that the scholar and the layman, the wise and the unwise, the old and the young, the man and the woman, all would understand it without any strain on the mind.

It is,however, strange to note that this Gospel also contains a high degree of science of religion, a beautiful style of expression, a high order of Divine Philosophy dealing with authoritative teaching of scriptures as well as certain unlogical differences, which show that all of it is the perfect word of God.

Here, we sould suggest our Christian Friends to think what is the basis for their accepting Jesus as Christ while the compilers of the four Gospels say that:

(a) he had no father
(b) his mother had no husband
(c) while in his blooming youth the house of Martha and Mary was open for him

(d) The pharisee had doubted his prophethood on this basis: "Now when the Pharisee which has bidden him saw it, he spoke within himself saying, this man if he were a prophet, would have known who and what manner of woman this is that toucheth him: for she is a sinner." (Luke 7:39).

(e) At the feast of *Tabernacles* the brothers of Jesus advised him to show his miracles at Jerusalem, but he refused to go there. But when his brothers were gone up, then went he also up into the feast, not openly, but as it were in secret. (John 7: 1—10).

(f) He was criticized for making wine and drinking it which he admitted.

(g) Celibacy recommended by him. (Matt.19:10—12).

(h) He received the Baptism of repentance from John the Baptist.

It is not our aim to criticize, but to say that the logic which you have used to prove Jesus as Christ and Prophet, if applied in relation with the Holy Prophet (p.b.u.h.), it would prove him worthier of his office as Prophet: That is to say that the very measures which prove Jesus as Christ or Prophet also prove the Holy Prophet as Prophet.

In a nut-shell, it is wrong to brand the Gospel of Barnabas as Muhammaden Gospel', as it was not within the reach of all. According to the Protestants, the Roman Church had confined the Bible so that none could read it. When Luther's friends for the first time, brought the Bible into public, people flocked to see it from all sides. So, when even the Christians were deprived of Bible, is it not rediculous to think that a Muslim has such a sound grip over it! Anyway, it is not possible that the Gospel of Barnabas was written by a person who was not aware of the teachings of the O.T. propnets or was not as perfect a scholar of the Latin Bible as a Monk. The Gospel of Barnabas gives the impression that its writer was a greater scholar of Christianity than of Islam. Hence, it is most probable that its writer was none other than Barnabas.

True it is that this Gospel includes certain narrations which are also found in Islamic literature. They are known as Semetics, but such narrations are regarded by Muslim Scholars as unauthentic. In fact, these are the narrations that were popular among the people of (Palestine).

Hark! is it not possible that the person who came across the Latin version of the Gospel of Barnabas should have written on the margins the reports that were commonly believed in, after having read in the Gospel the name of the Holy Prophet (p.b.u.h.), as the author himself can add to his writing, on the margins what he had forgotten to mention earlier, but he cannot write a comment on his own book. Hence, the writings on the margins probably belong to some Christian who believed in:

"For if the truth of God hath more abounded through my lie unto His Glory, why yet am I also judged as a sinner ---- Let us do evil, that good my come."

(*Romans.* 3:2,8)

According to the law of progressive revelation, the teaching of the Old Testament can be traced in the New Testament and finally in the Holy Qur'an duly amplified to enlighten the entire humanity for all the times to come. The guiding light of the Qur'an is to brighten the entire earth. It cannot be blamed for darkness if the fog of Pride and prejudice is in between. It has to benefit each and every person on earth and cannot be held liable if one hides himself in the dark of ignorance.

In the light of the Gospel according to St. Barnabas, it is for us to see whether we should still cling to the uncertain and obsolete tribal belief or to become an integral part of the great fraternity of Islam and help making the world free from destructive conflicts.

As for the style of Barnabas' Gospel, it is vivid, descriptive and circumstantial, yet the character of his Gospel is historical and apologetic, the order in which it proceeds is Geographical rather than Chronological.

The mission of the Apostle indeed, is not to be historian, but an apostle. For that purpose he selected, out of the Christ's teachings, such facts and words as were more suited to evoke and nourish the belief"in coming of the Lord." (Matthew 21:40). This selection was necessarily influenced by external and personal conditions of both the writer and those to whom his writings were addressed.

Yet, it was not occasioned by merely natural factors; the Apostle, in keeping with the doctrine of inspiration, was so moved by the Holy Ghost and impelled by Jesus Christ to write, that the things which he ordered, and these only; and finally expressed in apt words and with infallible truth. Hence, St.Barnabas was not the Chief author of his Gospel, he was but an instrument of the Holy Ghost. In this sense, the author is God Himself.

This is the main trend of the Gospel of Barnabas as it was originally delivered for Catechetical Instruction. The Christians should have received and welcomed it with open heart but, alas: this Divine Writ prejudiced and prompted them to declare it incredulous. In spite of the fact that:

(a) St. Barnabas' general Epistles were read in different churches; and

(b) The Gospel of Barnabas has a striking resemblance in so far as the Canonical Gospel shows the same general outline of the life and sayings of the Jesus Christ. Owing to differences in the three Synoptic narratives, St. Augustine explains, "There is no real disagreement, when one relates something which another does not mention, or expresses it in a different way; if these descriptions are put together they will combine to help and guide the reader in understanding the subject". (Epist, 199:25). The same is also true with regard to the Gospel according to St. Barnabas.

(c) The Apostle Barnabas was appointed by Jesus to write the Gospel. "And Jesus turned himself who writeth, and said, see, Barnabas, that by all means thou write my Gospel concerning all that hath happened through my dwelling in the world. And write in like manner that which hath befallen judas, in order that the faithful may be undeceived and every one may believe the truth" (Barnabas 222:1).

Now the question naturally arises why the Church did not canonize it. The answer is not a to seek. The Divine covenant had restricted the Prophethood in the descendants of Abraham only. This covenant was deliberately misinterpreted and the "Kingdom" and the "Prophethood" was wrongly believed to have been confined to the race of Isaac. The 'glad tiding' of the advent of Muhammad (p.b.u.h.) who belonged to the Ishmailites, prejudiced the church and prompted it to declare the Gospel of Barnabas in credulous. Otherwise, it surpasses the criterion set by the church for recognition of the four gospels. Had this Gospel been canonized, the Road to Mecca would have been open to all Christians by belief and the Church would have consequently been abdicated. Besides blocking the road to Mecca there is not a single trifling reason to ignore this **Gospel of Barnabas**

For conclusive proof that the Gospel according to Barnabas tells about Jesus Christ, his way of doing the Lord's work. Thus, it corroborates all the goodness of God which reveals Him in some aspect of His Character and dealings with mankind. It contains all the teachings of Jesus Christ as well as his ministerial Tours which have been presented most authentically. It cannot be denied:

(a) That St. Barnabas' general Epistles were read in different churches and

(b) That his Gospel gives more accurate, easy and comprehensible account of the Bible Land than either of the four Gospels.

(c) That it deals with all the life events of Jesus Christ according to time, i.e. historical and geographical aspects.

It is not difficult to trace the authenticity of Gospel of St. Barnabas with regard to its date, place and language. The general Epistles of St. Barnabas help immensely in this regard. In the light of his Epistles, it can be determined that Gospel according to Barnabas was written under the guiding spirit of Jesus. Its well-known and trustworthy Italian Text is safe in the Imperial Library of Vienna, the Capital of Austria. From among the persons, whose names history preserves, Mr. Cramer, Counsellor to the King of Prussia, was the first to get this Italian version in 1709 A.D. while he was in Amsterdam (Holland). It is however, not known when this gospel of Barnabas was transcribed in Italian Language and who did it?

False Measuring Stick:

How sad it is that every book dealing with life of Jesus in matophysical language is taken for a true Gospel. Four such Man-made accounts of the Gospel were officially

recognized by the Church and were included among the canonical scriptures. These four books are biographies. They do not give us a full account of all the deeds and sayings of Jesus Christ. Professor of St Mary's Theological College, Kurslong, says that "it is evident that we have not in our four Gospels, all the details about the life of Our Lord which one might wish to have and that we have no such biography of Jesus Christ. Yet we possess in our four forms of the "Gospel" all that we need in order to know that Jesus Christ is Our Saviour, Lord and God, and to believe in Him so as to obtain through that faith life ever............. lasting.........
(Cf. John. 20:31)"

(*Introduction of the Four Gospels in One Narrative*, P.X.).

In keeping with this general principle which we have quoted, "the preference has been given to the NARRATIVE which presents either the more personal characteristics of the Evangelist or which Portrays the personality of our Lord", says Professor of St. Mary's Theological College, Murseong.

With regard to Inspiration of the Gospel, the Professor further said that God, the author of theGospels, does not actually execute the writing miraculously; for this purpose He avails Himself of man as an instrument; He uses the very individuality of the hagiographer, his individual way of thinking, of expressing himself, his individual mentanlity. There is a very intimate co-operation between the action of God and the work of the hagiographer, God inspiring, influencing, building the free operation of His human instrument. In this way we understand quite well how God is the author of four Gospels, yet each has its own very pronounced character as regards contents, scope and style" (ibd. p. xii).

Matthew, Mark, Luke and John are all HUMAN. They are ALL subject to error. Even though they are directed, empowered and blessed by Him, He carried His work on through frail, weak HUMANS AND ALL HUMANS are subject to MISTAKES.

Any criterion that assumes God's TRUE WORK through humans is absolutely perfect, unable to be wrong or make mistakes or hold to any error, is a false measuring stick and therefore will be misleading.

Faulty Text:

St. Augustine mentions this, in a letter to St.Jerome "when in the pages of sacred writ, I came upon anyting that is contrary to the truth, I judged that the text is faulty, that the translation does not strike the right meaning or simply that I do not understand it".(Letter to St.Jerome IXXX 4,3)

Pope Les, xiii thus explains this divine authorship in his Encyclical on the Bible, Providentissimus Dues. He writes...... "The inspired writers are not mere passive instruments in their writings, but under the divine action are Intelligent, active and free agent".

We know that the author of the St. Luke Gospel consulted documents and gathered his facts from "eyes witnesses and ministers of the word" (Luke, 1:1,2). Therefore we often find verbal differences among them (see Matthew 5:3, compare with Luke 22:19, Mark 14:22, and 1 Cor. 11:23). Thus it need not be that every word of the Bible is dictated by God.

Now compare scripture with scripture, you will find, false doctrines, like false witness, agree not among themselves:); Let us here consider some of the obvious examples:

1. Jesus — the son of Joseph which was the son of Heli. (Luke, 3:23).

1. And Jacob begot Joseph, the husband of Marks of whom was born Jesus.:
(Math. 1:16).

2. When he arose, he took young child and his mother by night, and departed into Egypt; And was there until the death of Herod.
(Math. 22, 14,15).

2. And when they had performed all things according to the law of the Lord, they ventured into Gelles, to their own city, Nazereth.:
(Luke, 2:39).

3. Jesus came from Nazereth of Galilse, and was baptized of John in Jordan:
... And immediately the spirit driveth him into wilderness. And he was there in the wilderness forty days tempted of Satan.
(Mark, 1:9—13).

3. And the third day (after Jesus' baptism) there was a marriage in Cana of Galiles, and the mother of Jesus was there. And both of Jesus was called and made wine... This beginning of miracles did Jesus in Cana of Galilse.:
(John, 2:1—11).

4. And ye will not come to me that ye might have life. (John. 5.40)

4 No man can come to me, except the Father which hath sent me draw him.: (John: 6: 44).

5. Think not that I am come to send peace on earth I come not to send peacé, but a sword. (Matthew 10:34).

5. The word which God sent unto the children of Israel preaching peace by Jesus Christ. (Acts, 10: 36).

On earth peace, good will toward me. (Luke, 2: 14).

6. There is none other name under heaven given among men, whereby we must be saved. (Acts, 4:12).

6. In every nation be that feareth Him, and worketh righteousness, is accepted with him. (Acts, 10: 35).

7. And commanded them that they should take nothing for their journey, save a staff only. (Mark, 6: 8).

7. Provide neither gold, nor silver, nor brass in your purses, nor scrap for your journey neither two coats, neither shoes, nor yet staves. (Matthew 10: 9—10).

8. Think not that I am come to destroy the law, or the Prophets, but to fulfil. For verily I say unto you, till heaven and earth pass one jot or one title shall in no wise pass from the law, till all be fulfilled, Whosoever therefore shall break one of these least commandments and shall be called the least in the kingdom of heaven; but whosoever shall do and teach them, the same shall be called great in the kingdom of heaven.

(Matthew, 5: 17—19).

8. Whereof, my bretheren, ye also are become dead to the law by the body of Christ. (Rom. 7: 4).

Having abolished in his flesh the enmity, even the law of commandments contained in ordinaces. (Eph. 2: 15).

All that ever came before me are thieves and robbers. (John. 10: 8).

9. And it was the third hour and they crucified him.
(Mark 15:25).

10. And at the ninth hour Jesus cried... My God, why hast thou forsaken me?
(Mark, 15:34).

11. And they went out quickly, and fled from the sepulchre, for they trembled and were amazed; neither said they anything to any man, for they were afraid.
(Mark, 16:8).

12. For as many as have sinned without law shall also perish without law.
(Rom, 2:12).

13. For many are called, but few are chosen.
(Math. 22:14).

14. Whosoever is born of God doth not commit sin; because he is born of God.
(John, 3:9).

15. But he that shall blasphame against the Holy Ghost never forgiveness
(Mark, 3:29).

16. No man hath seen God at anytime. (John, 1:18) Whom no man hath seen, nor can see. (1 Tim. 6:16). God is a spirit(John 4:24).

9. About the sixth hour... they cried out. Away with him, away with him, crucify him. (John. 19:14—15).
10. I and my father are one.
(John. 10:30). For in him dwelleth all the fulness of the Godhead bodily.
(Col. 2:9).
11. And they remembered his words and returned from the sepulchre told all 'these things unto the eleven and to all the rest.
(Luke, 24:8,9).

12. For where no law is, there is no transgression.
(Rom, 4:14).

13. For it is written. As I live, saith the Lord, every knee shall bow to me, and every tongue shall confess to God. (Rom. 14:11).
14. There is none righteous, no not one.
(Rom. 3:10).

15. And by him all that believe justified from all things
(Acts, 13:39).

16. I saw the Lord standing upon the Altar. (Amos, 9:1). And the Lord appeared unto him. (Gen. 26:2).

17. With God all things are possible (Mark, 10:7). (Math, 19:26).

17. And he could there do no mighty work. (Mark, 6:5).

18. God is not a man that He should lie, neither the son of man that he should repent. (Numb. 23:19).

18. And it repented the Lord that he had made man on earth, and it grieved him at his heart. (Gen. 6:6).(Also Dent. 32:36; PS. 135:14).

19. Now the God of peace be with you all Amen, (Rom. 15:33)

19. The Lord is a man of war. (Ex. 15:3).

20. God is love. (1 John. 4:8).

20. God is a consuming fire. (Heb, 12:29).

21. Who will have all men to be saved, and to come unto the knowledge of the truth. (1 Tim, 2:4).

21. He hath blinded their eyes hardened their heart that they should not see with their eyes, nor understand with their heart, and also converted, and I should heal them. (John, 12:46).

Again, in Genesis 15:8, "Abraham is made to say, after receiving a promise of the Lord of Canaan: Lord God, whereby shall, I know that I shall inherit it." The sign given to Abraham according to Genesis 15:9—11 is quite meaningless, nor making clear how Abraham's seed was to inherit the Land. He said to him "Take me an heifer of three years old, and a she-goat of three years old, and a ram of three years old, and trutle dove, and a young pigeon. And he took urto him all these, and divided them in the midst, and laid each place one against another; but the birds divided he not. And when the fowls came down upon the carcases, Abraham drove them away." How was sign of Abraham inheriting the Land of Canaan is a mystry? It only shows that the text here has been tampered with. A book that contradicts itself can hardly be the word of God or an accurate account of the events it recalls in its narrative. The Bible is just such a book and is full of hopeless contradictions.

The Work of Man

On close examination, however, it must be admitted that in its present form it is the work of man. For instance, it may be safely quoted that Moses did not write the account of his own death in Deuteronomy 34 Chapter. The statement in Deuteronomy 1:1, that Moses spoke these words beyond Jordan is incidently made from the stand point of one living in Canaan, which Moses, never did. Other passages which can with difficulty be ascribed to him are: Exodus 6:26, 27:11:3; 16:35, 36: Numbers, 12:3; Deuteronomy, 2:12. In Genesis 14:14 and Deuteronomy 34: made of Dan, but the Territory did not rescue that name till it was conquered by the Danites, long after the death of Moses. (Josh, 19:47, Judges 18:29, 30).

Again, in Numbers 21:14, 15 there is quoted as an ancient authority the book of the Wars of the Lord", which plainly could not have been earlier than the days of Moses. Other passages which can with difficulty be ascribed to him are Ex. 6:26, 27; 11:3; 16:35,36; Lv. 18:24—26; Nu. 12:3, (Dummelow P. XXV) And again "A Careful examination has led many scholars to the conviction that the writings of Moses formed only the rough material or the part of the material, and that in its present form it is not the work of One man, but a compilation made from previously existing documents." (Dummelow, p. XXvi.).

According to the Renan, it is doubtful whether Moses was not a myth. Two versions of sacred history existed, different in language, style and spirit, and they were combined together into a narrative in the reign of Hezekiah (B.C. 727, 697). This forms the greater part of the Pentateusch as it exists today, excluding the greater part of Deuteronomy and Leviticus. In the reign of Josiah about 622 B.C. certain priests and scribes, with Jeremiah the Prophet, promulgated and a new code, pretending that they had found it in the Temple (2 Kings, 22:8).

This Law (Torah) was the basis of Judaism, the new religion then founded in Palestine. This was further completed by the sacrèdotal and Levetical Torah, compiled under the inspiration of Ezkiel, say, about 575 B.C., and contained mainly in the Book of Leviticus, with scattered fragments in Exodus, Numbers, and Joshua.

"We are entitled to accept the general results of a scientific examination of documents, probablities, and dates, even though we reject the premise which we believe to be false. viz, that God does not send inspired Books through inspired Prophets. We believe that Moses existed; that he was an inspired man of God; that he gave message which was afterwards distorted or lost; that attempts were made by Israel at various times to reconstruct that message; and that Torah, as we have it, is no earlier than the middle of fifth Century B.C."

Historical Facts

The aprocrayphal contains certain books which are not admitted as Canonical in the English Bible. But the early Christians received them as part of the Jewish scriptures, and the Council of Trent (A.D. 1545— 1563) seems to have recognized the greater part of them as canonical. The statements in 2 Esdras (about the first century A.D.) that the law was burnt and Ezra (say, about 458— 457 B.C.) was inspired to rewrite it, is probably true as to the historical fact that the law was lost, and that what we have now is no earlier than the time of Ezra, and some of it good later.

The Primitive Torah must have been in old Hebrew, but there is no Hebrew manuscript of the Old Testament which can be dated with certainty earlier than 916 A.D. Hebrew ceased to be a spoken language with the Jesus during or after the captivity and by the time we come to the period of Jesus, most cultivated Hebrew used the Greek languages and others used Aramaic including Syriac and Chaldee, Latin, or local dialects. There were also Arabic versions.. For historical purpose the most version were the Greek version, however as the Septuagint and the Latin version, known as the Vuigate. The septuagint was supposed to have been prepared by 70 or 72 Jews (Latin, Septuaginta- seventy) working independently and at different times, the earliest portion dating from about 284 B.C. This version was used by the Jews of Alexandria and the Hellenised Jews who were spread over all parts of the Roman Empire. The vulgate was a Latin translation made by the celebrated Father of the Christian Church St. Jerome from

Hebrew, early in the fifth century A.D. superseding the older Latin version. Neither the septuagint nor the vulgate have an absolutely fixed or certain text. The present standard text of the Vulgate as accepted by the Roman Catholic Church was issued by Pope Clement VIII (A.D. 1592—1605).

It will be seen therefore that there is no standard text of the Old Testament in its Hebrew form. The version differ from each other frequently in minor particulars and sometimes in important. It is in narrative form, and included the laws and regulations associated with the names of Moses, but probably compiled and edited from older sources by Ezra in the 5th Century B.C. As Renan remarks in the preface to his "History of the people of Israel", "the definite constitution of Judaism" may be dated only from the time of Ezra.

Authorities: Encyclopedia Britannica. "Bible".

(*Helps to the study of the Bible,* Oxford University press: A.F. Kerkpatric, *Divine Library of the Old Testament.* C.E. Hammond, *Outline of textual criticism;* E. Renon, *History of Israel;* G.F. Moore, *Literature of the Old Testament, and the Bibliography therein* (Home University Library);

Unreliable Record

The next of the New Testament is still more unrealiable. The writers of the Gospel report in Greek—the sayings of Jesus Christ who spoke Aramic. A copyist would sometimes put in not what was the text, but what he thought ought to be in it. He would trust a fickle memory, or he would even make the next with the view of the School to which he belonged.

As Prof. F.C. Burkitt remarks (Canon of the New Testament) it is an old miscellany. "The four biographies of Jesus Christ...... are not all independent of each other, and neither of them was intended by its writer to form one of quartette— But they are all put side by side, unharmonised, one of them being actually imperfected at the end, and one being only the first volume of a large work". All this body of unmethodical literature was casual in its nature. No wonder, because the early Christians expected the end of the world very soon. The four canonical Gospels were only four out of many, and some other besides the four have survived. Each writer just wrote down some odd sayings of the Master that the recollected. Among the miracles described there is only one which is described in all four canonical Gospels. Some of the Epistles contain expositions of doctrine, but this has been interpreted differently by different churches. There must have been hundred of such Epistles, and not all the Epistles, now received as canonical, were always so received or intended to be so received. The Apocalypse also was not the only in the field. There were others. They were prophecies of "things which must shortly come to pass"; they could not have been meant for long preservation for the time is at hand".

When were these four Gospels written? By the end of the second century A.D. (they were in existence, but it does not follow that they had been selected by that date to form a canon.) They were merely pious productions comparable to Dean Farrar's Life of Christ. There were other Gospels besides, And further, the writers of two of them, Mark and Luje, were not among the Twelve Disciples "Called by Jesus". About the Gospel of St. John there is much controversy as to authorship, date and even as to whether it was all written by one person. Clement of Rome (about 97 A.D.) and Polycarp (about 112 A.D.) quote sayings of Jesus in a form different from those found in the present canonical Gospels. Polycarp (Epistle, vii), inveighs much against men "who prevent the sayings of the Lord to their own lusts", and he wants to turn "to the word handed down to us from the beginning", thus referring to a Book (or a Tradition) much earlier than the four orthodox Gospels. An Epistle of St. Barnabas and an Apocalypse of St. Peter were recognised by Presbyter Clement of Alexandria (flourished about 180 A.D.) The Apocalypse of St. John, which is a part of the present canon in the West, forms no part of the peshitta (Ayriac) version of the Eastern Christians, which was produced about 411—413 A.D. and which was used by the Nestorian Christians. It is probable that the Peshitta was the version (or an Arabic form) used by the Christians in Arabic in the time of the Apostle. The final form of the New Testament Canon for the West was fixed in the fourth

Century A.D. (Say, about 367 A.D.) by Alhanasins and Nicane creed. The beautiful Codex Sinaiticus which was acquired for the British Museum in 1932, and is one of the earliest complete manuscripts of the Bible, may be dated about the fourth century. It is written in the Greek language. Fragments of unkonwn Gospels have also been discovered, which do not agree with the received canonical Gospels and in some others, of which traces survive (e.g. the Gospel of the childhood or the Notivity, the Gospel of St. Barnabas, etc.). Rightly spoken by the Quran that canonical Gospels are not the Gospel which revealed to Jesus, it was the single Gospel.

(Authorities: R.W. Mackay, *Rise and Progress of Christianity;* G.R.S. Mead, *the Gospel and the Gospels;* B.W. Bacon, *Making of the New Testament,* with its Bibliography; R. Hone, the *Apocryphal New Testament,* London 820; H.I. Bell and T.C. Skeat. *Fragments of an unknown Gospel and other Christian Papyri.)*

EPILOGUE

Before ending this book it is necessary to establish that the idea that the Gospel of Barnabas was written under the impression of Islamic point of view is not based on truth. Islam is not a new religion; it is the religion of all those prophets mentioned in the Bible. There is not a single prophet in Bible who taught (a) Trinity (b) That man is born in sin (c) and that no salvation is possible without atonement.

Hence, Moses says that (a) God is ONE (De. 6:4); Soloman says that (b) God created man upright "Lo, this only have I found, that God hath made man upright, but they have brought out many innovations" (Ecclesiastes 7:29).

Moses says that atonement is not required for salvation, and that it depends on the behaviour of each individual: "The fathers shall not be put to death for the children, neither shall the children be put to death for the fathers; every man shall be put to death for his own sin" (Deuteronomy, 24:16)).

Similarly, Jeremiah says: "But everyone shall die for his own iniquity; every man that eateth the sour grape, his teeth shall be set on edge" (Jeremiah, 31:30).

According to David, human sacrifice is a Devilish deed (Psalm, 106:37).

As a matter of fact, Saint Barnabas was a companion of Saint Paul. He knew that the attitude and behaviour of Saint Paul was in contrast with the mission of Jesus and that was distorting the teachings of Jesus Christ. Hence they parted asunder one from the other and he himself sailed for Cyprus. Obviously Paul had to get rid of a man as clever as Barnabas, not only because of the heresies, but also because Paul could not afford to mislead the latter. Jesus Christ ordered Barnabas to write the Gospel and he began to write the biography of Jesus under the guidance of the Holy Ghost.

Nowhere does Barnabas report Jesus as claiming Divinity or that God is Trinity and that he was one of the Persons of Trinity, being His son. Nor did he ever hear that Jesus Christ had come to atone for the sins of mankind. The truth is that it was all the innovation of Saint Paul.

Incidentally, the current Gospels do not prove that God is Trinity or that Jesus died to atone for the sins of mankind. Saint John, however, wrote in his Gospel in the style of Christ: "I and my father are one". (John, 10:30). These words are further explained in his prayer: "Holy Father! keep through Thine own Name those whom Thou hast given me, that they may be one and I in Thee, that they also may be one in us; that the world may believe that Thou hast sent me"—(John, 17:11, 21, 22).

These verses eloquently show the fact that the unity that is expressed therein is not physical or personal, it is, on the contrary, spiritual, even as that which exists between God and the devotee. The same idea is expressed in the remarks of Jesus: "My Father is greater than I" (John 16:28). Had he been Divine, he would never have said that Father was greater than he. Once Jesus described himself as a 'door' and no Christian did ever take him for a door made out of iron or timber. Similarly, he has also described himself as a vine (grape tree) and none did ever take him for a tree. In fact, these are metaphorical expressions meant to convey the idea of particular relationship.

There still remains the question that the Gospel of Barnabas differs from other Gospels in relation with certain details. One of these differences is relating to a prophet that was to come after Jesus Christ, and whose name, according to Barnabas, was to be Muhamamd Rasul-ul-Lah. The writers of the other Gospels have also mentioned a prophet that was to come after Jesus. The difference exists only in relation with the name that Barnabas has mentioned. It is now clear that the rejection of the Gospel of Barnabas proceeds from the grudge for the Holy Prophet, and the rest of their argument consist of mere pretentions.

Solomon has named the prophet that was to come "MUHAMMADIM". In Hebrew the suffix "im" is used to express respect, as the term "Eloha" which means "God" is mentioned in Bible as "Elohim". It is thus clear that Solomon has quite distinctly mentioned the name of the prophet that was to come as "MAHAMAD". But an error is made, intentionally or un-intentionally, by translating the proper name as "Altogether Lovely". Even the translation "Altogether Lovely' is a befitting attribute of the Holy

Prophet, as mentioned in the words of Hadith. The Hebrew words in Roman script are as follows:

HIKKO MAMITTAQIM VIKULLO MAHAMADDiM ZEH DUDI VEZEW RAAI BENUTE YARUSHALAM

The English translation thereof is as follows:
"His mouth is most sweet; yet, hc is Mohamad altogether lovely. This is my beloved and this is my friend, O daughter of Jerusalem!"

Finally, let us add that if the Gospel of Barnabas is rejected only because it contains more more material, the execuse does not sound plausible, as it is not a defect to contain more material. Matthew has described in his Gospel a number of such details which are not to be found in other Gospels. The 'sermon of the Mount' which is the very life of Christianity, is mentioned by Luke in a few scattered sentences, while Mark and John have dropped it altogether from mentioning. Who is, then responsible for this short coming? Is it Matthew or Mark and John, who have ignored such an important teaching? Is it then right to treat Matthew as guilty of the additional report and reject his Gospel on that account?

However, there is no doubt about the fact that the compiler of the Gospel of Barnabas was a philosopher and writer of great merit. The most outstanding merit of the Gospel of Barnabas is that it contained glamourous signs of wisdom; a beautiful style of description relating to good manners and moral sublimity. The simplicity and easy flow of the language renders it still more pleasant to read. It aims at rousing the sentiments for the purification of the soul. It enjoins righteousness and warns against evil; enjoins the cultivation of good habits and warns against meanness; it inspires the reader with the love of God and the love of man calls upon him to cultivate the habit of self denial, resulting in the eradication of pride and selfishness, so that one may willingly endow ones own life for the betterment and uplift of others.

The Gospel of Barnabas contains a complete history of Jesus Christ from his birth to his ascension, and most of the circumstances in the four Gospels are to be found therein.

The difference, however, consists in that (a) whereas Barnabas has named the prophet that was to come as Muhammad, the canonical Gospels mention him in the metaphorical language as 'Paraclete' or the comforter, i.e., Ahmad (b) while Barnabas has denied the death of Jesus Christ at the cross, the canonical Gospels have condemned such death as an accursed one. Hence Jesus Christ had prayed that he might be saved from such an end, and his prayer was responded to. Consequently, the facial features of Jesus Christ were altered and yet another person who was really an accursed one was crucified in his place. The lookers on thought that the person crucified was Jesus Christ, but it was a mere delusion (c) while Barnabas asserts that salvation depends on acts of' righteousness, the canonical Gospels declare that it depends on the Living Faith, that is, putting faith into practice or faith aided by acts of righteousness. As a matter of fact, it is only a verbal difference, while the meaning remains the same; and the truth is that salvation depends on the practice of righteousness (d) While Barnabas asserts the Unity (oneness) of God, the canonical Gospels metaphorically mention Jesus Christ as the son of God. It, however, depends on individual understanding.

As a matter of fact, there were a large number of sects during the Apostolic Age, among whom there were two that particularly debated over the personality of Christ. One of these sects was the 'Irenaem' that was unitarian and had belief in one God, while the other sect 'Paulin Brant' was Trinitarian, and was largely composed of non-jews. The former sect viewed Christ as human who ate, drank and lived even like other humans, while the latter claimed that he was Divine in the form of man. The famous 'Nicene council' met in 325 CE to settle the dispute between these two sects, and the 'Paulists' succeeded in having their belief recognised purely by the strength of their majority. The unitarians, however, have stuck to their belief upto this day.

The Councils of Nicaea and Locodicea were held about 350 years after the time Christ is said to have lived; and the books that now compose the New Testament were then voted for by YEAS and NAYS, as we now vote a law. As great many that were offered had a majority of NAYS, and were rejected. This is the way the New Testament came into being. (Age of Reason p. 92, by Thomas Paine).

No body in the whole history of Christianity has been able to give a rational explanation of the doctrine of Trinity, No man in his senses can accept it and not even a believing Christian with any sense of decency and propriety can have the courage now to argue for it.

God being the unseen, He cannot incorporate Himself in any visible form, He cannot take upon Himself the form of a man and descend into our midst because the moment He does so, He ceases to be unseen, and when He ceases to be unseen and becomes visible, man cannot worship Him in spirit, because a visible thing can be worshipped with the body and by those only who see it.

Jesus Christ throughout the Gospels and the Qur'an is spoken of as a mortal being, therefore, it is an error, to take him for God. Since he was conceived by a woman in the manner in which all women conceive he was fed as children are fed, he ate food and drank water and answered the calls of nature. Then how can it be true that Jesus was with God or Son of God? The likeness of Jesus with God is truly as the likeness of Adam. He created him from dust, then said to him "BE" and he was" (Al-Quran, iii-58).

May our readers find, in the study of this Gospel of St. Barnabas, what we have found in the preparation of it, an ever-enlarging, knowledge of, and an ever-deepening reverence for the WORD which, "inspired of God, is also profitable for teaching for reproof, for correction, for instruction which is in righteousness; that the man of God may be complete, furnished completely unto every good work".

WHY CONFLICT?

The Source of St. Barnabas

Here, it seems necessary to make it celar that the idea that the author of the Gospel of Barnabas was a Jew by birth who had embraced Christianity first and later on embraced Islam, is a baseless assumption. But even if this assumption is adopted, it is not possible to deny the authenticity of Barnabas which is based not on the personality of the writer but on the inspiratio' under which he wrote the Gospel. The gift of the Holy Ghost, as we know, was not confined to the apostles alone: none had an exclusive claim over it.

Hence we read in 'Acts of the Apostles' that this gift of the Holy Ghost did not come to any one as his exclusive right, nor is it a matter that can be had at will, it rather depends on Him who confers it, and what God wills, He grants it and His grant is unlimited.

"Then Peter opened his mouth and said:

By a truth I perceive that God is no respecter of persons....... while Peter yet spoke these words, the Holy Ghost fell on all them which heard the word. And they of the circumcision which believed were astonished, as many as came with Peter, because that on the Gentiles also was poured out the gift of Holy Ghost."[67] (Acts, 10:34,44,45).

So, when we read the Gospel of Barnabas it becomes clear to us that the source of its power and light is God Himself. God had conferred upon the writer of Barnabas the gift of the Holy Ghost with a definite purpose, i.e. to conduct His word to us which He had revealed to Jews, and spread the Light which He had conferred upon Jews. It is so because Matthew, Mark, Luke and John were influenced by the Greek Philosophy and had stationed Jesus in the rank of the Greek gods. Thus did the Greek mythology took the place of Theology in the Church. God, however, willed to preserve the honour of His Name, hence He granted the Church a person who was well known to it: who said:

---

67. *Acts of the Apostles* 10:34,44,45.

"God is hidden, He is one, He has no peer, He has no beginning and no end. God is greatest, He is abstracted from all created things, there is none to compose Him, neither is he compounded of things. He is one God, the Eternal God."

This is the teaching of the prophets of Bible which Barnabas heard from Jesus and recorded. If you compare the Bible with the Gospel of Barnabas you will certainly pronounce Barnabas as a prophet of God whom He had chosen for a particular service, in order that the truth may be separated from falsehood and the pure milk from water. Hence, the claim that the Gospel of Barnabas was written by a false pretender under the former's name is a baseless assumption with no historical proof to back it. God who could create progeny for Abraham out of stones (Luke 3:8) is not bound to do His will in accordance with the views of the Church. Nor can Church bind the Hands of God. If the teachings of Barnabas had been in contrast with the teachings of the earlier prophets the objections would have demanded our attention. Our criterion is not the New Testament, it is the Old Testament which was quoted by Jesus himself and which he had regarded as a source of guidance — the real teachings of Jesus especially when contradictions and anomalies are found there in abundance. There is no doubt that those Gospels were compiled in democratic methods of Greeks, they cannot therefore be the words and sayings of Jesus for his language was Aramaic, and of the Gospels it is Greek.

Referring to the objections raised against the present Gospel of Barnabas, I can say that all those and more can truly and safely be applied to all the those four Gospels.

Jesus taught nothing more or less to his people, nothing else than the teaching of the prophets appeared earlier to him. The four Gospels however contain matter contrary to the teachings of the earlier prophets.

Where is the original Gospel of Barnabas? No one in his senses ever flogs a dead donkey, you cannot ban a Gospel that does not exist. The Gospel of St. Barnabas must have been very verily to survive condemnation. Since the vested interests of Christianity are asked to produce the condemned version from time to time. Thus the duty of the Christian Church is to inform the world as to what they have done to that Gospel.

The Clarendon Press is, however, to be thanked for their printing and publishing this Gospel and thereby presenting a rare book to the readers of the world. It recalls to our minds Moses who was brought in to the household of the Pharaoh· who was, later on, to save the nation and to convey the glad — Tidings of one "like unto thee" was similar unto Moses (The Holy Prophet Muhammad.)

(Deuteronomy 18:18).

In the *Encyclopaedia Britannica,* under the heading "Apocryphal Literature" is an entry.

Gospel of Barnabas condemned in the Gelasian Decree. Decretum Gelasianum is described as a compilation of documents anterior to St. Gregory (C540—C604) and it is difficult to determine Gelasius contribution to it, and at all events as we know it, it is of Roman origin and sixth Century or later". Gelasius is explained as "Gelasius, St., confirmed the estrangement between the eastern and western churches by insisting on the removal of the name of Acacius, bishop of Constantinopole, from the deptychs".

In the first place, if the Gelasian Decree is anterior to St. Gregory, who died at 604 then it cannot be 'later' than the sixth century except by a maximum of four or five years. In any case it would be anterior to Islam, which was not born till 623 CE, much later than even circa 604. In the second, if the Gospel of St. Barnabas was "condemned in the Gelasian Decree", then how can a document which had been condemned before Islam was born, be forged by a Muslim convert nine hundred years later, in the fifteenth century?

The truth seems to be that as Unitarian Gospel of Barnabas did not suit the Trinitarian Christian Creed adopted at the Council of Nicaea (325 CE) and confirmed at the council of Constantinople (381 CE)., the Gospel has been given a 'bad name' and 'hanged' first in the Decree of Gelasius in the sixth Century, and then, not content with even this, its writer dubbed a "renegade" and a "forger", a convenient Peg on which to hang its authorship. That St. Barnabas did write a Gospel is admitted by Christian chroniclers themselves, e.g. in John Talenets Nazareunis

(1718 or, Jewish, Gentile and Mahometan Christianity, containing the history of the ancient Gospel of Barnabas and the modern Gospel of Mohametans attributed to the same apostle". The only one actually available in the world today is apparently a forgery of the fifteenth century; then where is the one really written by Barnabas, the "Ancient" one and, mind you, condemned not later than the sixth century? "Lost" after the usual pattern, via, "condemnation? Quite obviously, Christendom, whose disregard of history is now too well known to critical scholarship, could not sterm the truth stated in Barnabas, and therefore brought the same disregard of history to bear on this Gospel (*Christianity in History*, pp. 30—32).

MUHAMMADAN GOSPEL

At this juncture, we shall deal with the theory of MUHAMMADAN GOSPEL, which was condemned before the birth of Islam. However it is inconceiveable that the Gospel of such a great Apostle should have been denied the honour of inclusion in canon of the New Testament. Prejudices die hard. This Gospel disagreed with the preconceived notions of the early Christian Church, and thus it was condemned.

No one in his senses ever flogs a dead donkey. You cannot ban a Gospel that does not exist. The Gospel of St.Barnabas must have been very virile to survive condemnations. Since the vested interests of Christianity are reluctant in accepting the Vienna Manuscripts as authentic they must be asked to produce the condemned version form time to time. Thus it is the duty of the Christian Church to inform the world as to what they have done to that Gospel?

However, it is not easy for the common man to make independent research on this subject, and because the pet objection to the Muslim viewpoint on the crucifixion is based on the fallacy that the testimony of the Holy Prophet (peace be upon him) coming six hundred years after the event and a thousand miles from the scene of happening should not be considered as against the evidence of eye-witnesses at the time of the occurrence", it would be futile, because of the existing bias in the Christian mind, to advance the metaphysical aspect of Qur'anic information that God spoke through His Servant Muhammad (peace be upon him) Therefore I proved from the New Testament itself that Jesus Christ was NEITHER KILLED NOR CRUCIFIED as the Jews boasted and Christians believed.

THE SOURCES OF CHRISTIAN CHURCH

The great Greek philosophers — Socrates, Plato, Zeno, Aristotle, Epicurus — had a profound effect on Christian religion. The ancient gods decline in importance after their time. Creater freedom of conscience became the rule. Oriental mystery religions were easily introduced, and, as we have seen, they became very prolific. Into such an era came Christianity with all the advantages and most of the attributes of the other Eastern religions, and a higher ethic than any of them.

Christianity in common with the mystery cults the idea that man could "get right with God". There was a Saviour God, who had become a man to teach mankind a way of life, who had died, who had been resurrected, and through whom those who had faith would be saved. Christianity offered greater consolation and held out the promise of a more exalted and beautiful future existence. Much that was Pagan, Oriental, or foreign to Christianity was adapted in whole or in part to the new religion. From the East came conventional architecture, mosaic arrangements of figures, the use of the halo and incense (it was due to the use of these Eastern attributes that the Christian Church evnetually broke in two — the Roman Church and the Greek Church). From Judaism, Christianity adopted the idea of fatherhood of God and the idea of Christian love, mercy, and justice. From the Greeks came many philosophical ideas —" THE WORD" "THE LOGOS", "THE GODHEAD". To the Greek, word had the same attributes as gods, for they could be used over and over without ever wearing out, but rather growing in strength and meaning with use. The Roman contribution was late in coming, but not less important — Romans gave Organisation.